ENCOUNTERS

Meditations and Prayers

Twilight *Watercolour*

Eddie Askew

By the same author:
A Silence and A Shouting
Disguises of Love
Many Voices One Voice
No Strange Land
Facing the Storm
Breaking the Rules
Cross Purposes
Slower than Butterflies
Music on the Wind
Edge of Daylight (Memoirs)
Talking with Hedgehogs (book and spoken word cassette)
Unexpected Journeys
Love is a Wild Bird (book and spoken word cassette)

Published by
The Leprosy Mission International
80 Windmill Road, Brentford
Middlesex TW8 0QH, United Kingdom

First published 2004

Editorial and Design by Craft Plus Publishing Ltd.
53 Crown Street, Brentwood, Essex CM14 4BD
Printed and bound in Spain by Bookprint, S.L. - Barcelona

A catalogue record for this book is available from the British Library.
ISBN 0 902731 54 8

Cover picture (printed in full on pp 56-57): Under the Trees, South Africa, *Watercolour*

Contents

Dedication

To The Leprosy Mission's field workers,
both national and expatriate,
who live out their faith
at the sharp end

Foreword

Another new book by Eddie Askew is always worth waiting for and no doubt this will be another bestseller! In *Encounters* Eddie enables us to step inside the life of five Bible characters, and to imagine their personal encounter with Jesus first-hand.

Eddie transports us back to Bible times. His well-chosen words and observations will take you right into the heart of the situation, while his paintings will delight your eye and contribute to the rich sense of atmosphere.

Perhaps the Bible passages will be familiar, but Eddie's writing is always fresh and full of new insights. You might even be left asking yourself, "Why didn't I think of that before?" Every Bible study is complemented with a prayer that is both poetic and down-to-earth – quite an achievement in itself.

As a surgeon I have particularly enjoyed re-reading the healing miracles of Jesus described within these pages. Eddie brings us the paralysed man, who gains the power to walk, the blind man who discovers the beauty of God's creation, and the man with leprosy who is restored to full health. Add to these the stories of Mary at the tomb and doubting Thomas (or honest Thomas as Eddie calls him) and you have a range of studies that challenge, inspire and encourage. Take each of the sections in this book one at a time and perhaps you too will encounter Jesus through these meditations and prayers.

I warmly commend this book to you.

Professor the Lord McColl
President of the Council of The Leprosy Mission England and Wales

Introduction

Writing doesn't come easily. This book has been a struggle – not so much a struggle to write, more a struggle to listen. To listen to the words on the Bible page; spoken words reduced to paper. To hear the tone in which they were originally spoken. To listen to my own imagination; and to hear through all these activities the sound, sometimes faint, sometimes loud and challenging, of the Spirit at work.

The insights, if any, are his. The mistakes are mine. But that is how we grow – through insight and mistake, relying on the ever-present, ever-patient love of God to guide and correct, and redirect our steps.

May you enjoy reading this book at least half as much as I have enjoyed the struggle of writing it.

Eddie Askew

Morning Light, Lake District

Part One

"The man who made me well..."

Watercolour

Reading - John 5:1-15

Some time later, Jesus went up to Jerusalem for a feast of the Jews. Now there is in Jerusalem near the Sheep Gate a pool, which in Aramaic is called Bethesda and which is surrounded by five covered colonnades. Here a great number of disabled people used to lie – the blind, the lame, the paralysed – *and they waited for the moving of the waters. From time to time an angel of the Lord would come down and stir up the waters. The first one into the pool after each such disturbance would be cured of whatever disease he had.* One who was there had been an invalid for 38 years. When Jesus saw him lying there and learned that he had been in this condition for a long time, he asked him, "Do you want to get well?"

"Sir," the invalid replied, "I have no-one to help me into the pool when the water is stirred. While I am trying to get in, someone else goes down ahead of me."
Then Jesus said to him, "Get up! Pick up your mat and walk." At once the man was cured; he picked up his mat and walked.

The day on which this took place was a Sabbath, and so the Jews said to the man who had been healed, "It is the Sabbath; the law forbids you to carry your mat."
But he replied, "The man who made me well said to me, "Pick up your mat and walk."
So they asked him, "Who is this fellow who told you to pick it up and walk?"
The man who was healed had no idea who it was, for Jesus had slipped away into the crowd that was there.

Later Jesus found him at the temple and said to him, "See, you are well again. Stop sinning or something worse may happen to you." The man went away and told the Jews that it was Jesus who had made him well.

* * *Text between two asterisks is only included in some manuscripts.*

Imagine...

Light and shade. The glare of the sun is harsh. It bounces off the white walls of the five colonnades. They surround the pool, one on each of the four sides, the fifth running down the middle, dividing the pool into two. Coming out of the sunlight, eyes take a moment to adjust to the shade under the arches. There are people everywhere, crowding and pushing. This is no ordinary gathering. There are many people with disabilities. Some lame, moving slowly and painfully on their sticks. Others can't move at all. They sit with their backs propped against the pillars of the colonnades. Some are prostrate, lying full length on mats. Others are blind. Some have companions with them, people who still care, but many are alone. Alone in the crowd. Alone with illness and pain and deprivation. There are beggars, living rough, hoping for nothing more than a crust of bread, a shelter from the cold night.

A child cries and is comforted by anxious parents hoping for a miracle, for an end to pain and suffering. Others lie quietly, just waiting, as they wait each day, tides of hope and disappointment flowing and ebbing through their lives. It's a restless assembly. There's a continual shuffling as people change places, move in and out through the arches. The atmosphere is hot and stuffy; little breeze penetrates the densely packed space. The air is full of the smells of poverty and illness. These are poor people, marginalised, always living on the fringes.

The noise is constant too. A murmur of conversation underlies raised voices and the occasional sound of protest and argument as individuals try to protect their personal space. There's anger too as others elbow their way deeper into the gathering, determined to get nearer to its centre.

And there, surrounded by the arcades, is the reason. Two pools of water, the focus of attention. In contrast to the crowd, the water is still and clear and cool, its surface undisturbed. Those with the strength and determination elbow their way to the water's edge and wait. The nearer people get to the water, the quieter and more watchful they become. No-one knows when it will next move and bubble. They must be ready. The mood is a mixture of waiting, expectation and tension.

Now there is in Jerusalem near the Sheep Gate a pool. Which in Aramaic is called Bethesda and which is surrounded by five covered colonnades. Here a great number of disabled people used to lie - the blind, the lame, the paralysed - and they waited for the moving of the waters.

John 5:2-3

It was a last-hope place full of last-hope people. Bethesda means 'House of Grace', or 'House of Mercy'. Ironic really, as we imagine the scene. The tension was there all the time. These were people who had tried everything; who'd gone through the misery of illness and pain. Folk who'd prayed, made their offerings at the temple – although many who were physically disabled weren't welcome there anyway. "Now," they said, "we've tried everything else, let's try the waters."

A few were still optimistic, others despaired, and I'm sure there were sceptics too. Most people believed that when the water in the pool swirled and bubbled the first person into the water would be cured, whatever the illness. But the water was unpredictable. You had to be ready for the next disturbance and no-one knew when that would be. It made Bethesda an aggressive, competitive place. People were alert for the opportunity, ready to move, to plunge in before anyone else. There must have been many false starts as people jumped to be first in the water; argument and anger as short-tempered sufferers crowded the margins of the pool. There was little love for neighbours and their needs, and deep disappointment when nothing happened. And cruel laughter when some unfortunate got a pointless soaking.

There wasn't much medical hope for people with serious or chronic illness. There were physicians in Jerusalem but most were available only for those who could pay. Even for them choices were limited. Herbal remedies, poultices, wine and oil, diets – and time. Waiting patiently sometimes works but it's hard to tell that to the poor, the blind, the paralysed. And as a last resort there were opiates as a temporary relief from pain. There was also something many invalids know – the frustration of what Angela Ashwin* calls the humiliation of being helpless – their agenda set by their illness and their carers, and being unable to decide for themselves what to do or when and where to go.

* Pain into Prayer *by Angela Ashwin, published by Fount, 1997*

Then Jesus walks in, quietly, unobtrusively and unrecognised. R.S. Thomas, the Welsh Christian poet, writes of this quiet coming of Christ:

As I had always known
he would come, unannounced,
remarkable merely for the absence
of clamour *

That's often the way with Jesus. His humility may sit uneasily on the shoulders of more aggressive Christians today but, recognised or not, he's abroad in our world. He stands unidentified, unseen, among the disadvantaged and the poor, and comes to those at the back of the queue. He asks no privileges. And he breaks the rules when they get in the way of compassion. Yet with his coming, one life is about to change dramatically.

* Suddenly *from* Collected Poems *1945 –1990, published by Phoenix*

Lord, you come into my life
so quietly.
No banners, big parades
or high street demonstrations.
At times I hardly know you're there.
You hover on the wind of my attention,
your patience infinite,
ready to dip a wing and glide,
slide into my consciousness
without a sound.
You wait,
until I find a moment in my oh-so-busy life
to turn to you.
And then you swoop
and, feather-light,
I feel the warm enfolding of your love.
There's no reproach –
I sometimes think
I'd rather be rebuked
at my unfaithfulness
than welcomed unconditionally
the way you do –
but that's your nature
and I'm reassured
that though you're often
out of sight and earshot
you're always present in my life.
You know my needs
and when I look to you,
your love can make me whole.

One who was there had been an invalid for 38 years.
John 5:5

I see the man in my imagination. He's lying on a worn and dusty mat, his back propped against a pillar. He has a stick and a little bundle of possessions by his side, an earthenware drinking cup and a begging bowl. How else would he survive? He's gaunt and thin, muscles wasted and weak. He finds it difficult to move. Lines of pain etch a picture of misery and despair into his face. His eyes are dull and without expression.

We don't know what was wrong with him. Perhaps it was the result of an accident or a birth defect; maybe polio or some other form of paralysis. I feel his early days of suffering, when anger burned in his mind. Anger at the unfairness of the world he lived in, the injustice that picked him out for pain. Anger against a society which pushed him to its margins and abandoned him. Anger too against God who had allowed this to happen, although being angry with God is harder to face and admit. Many of us feel we mustn't be angry with God, that somehow it isn't allowed, and so we suppress it. But anger with God is often expressed in the Bible. It's not unusual. Psalm 44 is an angry reproach to God from a people in deep trouble, and there are many similar passages. There are moments of stress when we say, "I'm so angry I can't pray." Yet this is the time we most need to pray, to confront our anger, to let it out and find release. God has a remarkable capacity for surviving our anger and not holding it against us. There's hidden anger in all of us that needs to be faced and dealt with. Find a critic, one who can so easily point out the faults in other people, and you'll find buried anger.

But back to the invalid. I hear him asking, "What have I done to deserve this? Why me? Why have I been singled out?" And underlying the desperate questions was the Jewish belief that everything, including his pain and helplessness, came directly from God. "There is no suffering without sin," said the rabbis, their dogmatism adding to his feeling of injustice the burden of believing that God was punishing him for his sinfulness. It made it all his own fault. A heavy burden to bear. "If God is for us, who can be against us?" proclaimed St. Paul later, writing to Christians in Rome (Romans 8:31), but the invalid might have groaned, "If God is against us, who can be for us?" What hope could he cling to? He had no expectations any more.

Thirty-eight years is a long time to be ill; to be living on the edge, not only of the pool, but also of life. I take 38 years off my age and think of all I've experienced and achieved in that great chunk of my life, including the mistakes – and if taking 38 years off your life leaves you yet to be conceived and born then think of your whole life lived like that. All this he has lost. All this he has had to endure. And he's alone. We don't know how he managed to drag himself to Bethesda but he tells Jesus, "I have no-one to help me." There's despair in the simple comment. Neither do we know how Jesus picked him out in the crowd. Somehow his need spoke for him.

Jesus shoulders his way through the gathering and pauses. He stands and looks down at the sick man. Then I see Jesus in one quick movement crouch down beside him, getting on his level, eye to eye. How long would it have been since anyone did that? Jesus sees the man, not as a 'client' as modern medical jargon has it today – an honest if clumsy attempt to bridge the sometimes patronising gap between helper and helped – but as a friend.

In that moment, wholeness confronts brokenness. The *shalom*, the harmony, of Jesus faces the disharmony, the dis-ease, of the invalid. Jesus concentrates all his attention and love on him. It's a moment of great intensity. The power of God focusing through Jesus onto the personality and need of one weak human being. Reaching out to him, and through him to all of us. That's what God has done in Jesus – come down to human level to offer healing to the whole of wounded creation. We all share the wounds, the disappointments and dashed hopes of our world, but his presence offers the healing we long for, even when we can't articulate it. The reality of grace is ready to transform the gracelessness of Bethesda, the House of Grace.

Lord,
You came into the desert of his life
like sunlight through a lens,
your energy bright-focussed
on the desiccated tinder of his pain.
You came
to set his life on fire with love.
To raise him
from his bed of loneliness
and invite him to reach out
and take the healing only you could offer.

"No-one to help," he said.
I know the feeling, Lord.
The times when life looks dark and bleak
and when I reach for you I find no touch,
no point of contact,
merely an empty space
which you once occupied.
Yet you are near,
my life's experience says it's so,
and I just need to wait
for clouds to lift
and let the sunshine through.

The waiting's hard,
however long or short the time,
but when I think my strength has gone
and I am ready to give up,
I glimpse you walking
through the crowd
of my preoccupations
to stand,
a presence by my side.
And then I know
the healing can begin.

Towards Mull, from Iona

Watercolour

When Jesus saw him lying there and learned that he had been in this condition for a long time, he asked him, "Do you want to get well?"

John 5:6

One thing among many that irritate me is being given a long-winded answer to a simple question. Maybe I still need to learn that some questions are not as simple as they seem and that it's often easier to ask a question than to give an answer. Jesus comes straight to the point. "Do you want to get well?" he asks softly. At first thought this was a simple question. The man had somehow struggled to Bethesda and tried to get to the water so the answer was obvious. Yet he doesn't give a straight answer. Instead of a simple yes he pours out his problems. He has no-one to help – he had, although he didn't know it – and someone else always got to the water first. Why was he alone? Where were his family? Had they abandoned him? Had he no friends? Surely he'd want to change all this?

On the face of it he would like to get well. Don't we all when we're ill? But I sense anxiety as he hears the question. Difficult though it was, his life was the only one he'd known for 38 years. It was unpleasant but it was predictable. He'd come to terms with its limitations. The threadbare mat he lay on was his world and his security, and his horizons had contracted to the view from there. He'd given up. Surrendered, and who could blame him? How long can you fight? He knew his place and to leave it would be to face the uncertainty of change. It would demand that he take on the responsibility of carving out a new life for himself. "Do you want to get well?" meant, "Are you prepared to change?" Could he find the courage to face an unknown future? A much more difficult question to answer, but it's one that Jesus asks us all.

I remember a visit to South Korea, years ago. The folk I stayed with had a watchdog, large and black. It was well fed and had a comfortable outdoor kennel. It was attached to it by a long lead, which gave it a limited freedom within the backyard. One day I suggested to my host that we take the dog with us when we went for a walk. He hesitated, then unfastened the lead, but the dog wouldn't take a single step outside the garden. It became anxious, crouched and whining, its tail down. Nothing would persuade it to move out. The yard and kennel, even the long lead which controlled it, had become its security. It was only comfortable in its own tiny world. Freedom, venturing into the unknown, seemed to mean danger.

Perhaps it was similar for the lame man. The freedom Jesus offers can be frightening. It's a call to uncertainty, a challenge to face a new reality, new relationships. Living with Jesus isn't an easy option. But Jesus releases us from 'the paralysis of our inhibitions', as Anselm Gruen says,* and offers us the opportunity to take responsibility for our own lives.

Jesus wastes no time. Many people would see the man as a hopeless case, set in his ways and incapable of change, but not Jesus. He challenges the man to find his real self, the self overlaid by sickness and fear. "You can do it," he says, "You can. Come on, get on your feet." Now their eyes meet and hold. There's an exchange of feeling, a sense of power moving from the one to the other. Jesus wills the man to respond and take part in his own healing. He must want it for himself. "Pick up your mat," Jesus tells him, his whole will concentrated on the man. "Make an effort. At least do that for yourself." The man gathers strength, takes a deep breath and, still looking at Jesus, he picks up his mat and walks. His first steps are short and hesitant, the next stronger, more certain. It's a resurrection moment, when new life becomes a reality for him and he is released from the tomb of his own fears.

* Images of Jesus, *by Anselm Gruen, published by Continuum, 2002*

Lord, you scare me
with your expectations.
You offer more
than I'm prepared to take.
I'm comfortable, lying here.
I know just where I am.
There may be more creative ways of living
and more adventure just around the corner
but they would call for effort
I'm not prepared to give.
Freedom may sound attractive
– bright dreams of what could be –
but something holds me back.
I would say yes,
reach out and grasp
the healing in your hands.
But timid as I am
I find it hard
to loose my hold on certainties,
roll up the mat I cling to
and walk out into liberty.

Your universe of love expands,
extends beyond the furthest boundaries
of my imagination.
The height and breadth and depth of love
too big, too wonderful for me.
I'm overwhelmed.
I think that if it were a little less
it would be easier to accept.
Yet as I look into your eyes
I'm drawn to take a first small step.
I ask you, Lord,
with all the courage I can harvest
from my life,
to take my hand.

Release me from the tomb of my timidity.
Help me to find a resurrection moment,
that wondrous metamorphosis,
when new life
splits the hard cocoon of fear
in which I've lived.

And let me learn that my security
rests not in what I know
but in your presence
wherever you may lead.
And suddenly I'll find my legs
and walk.

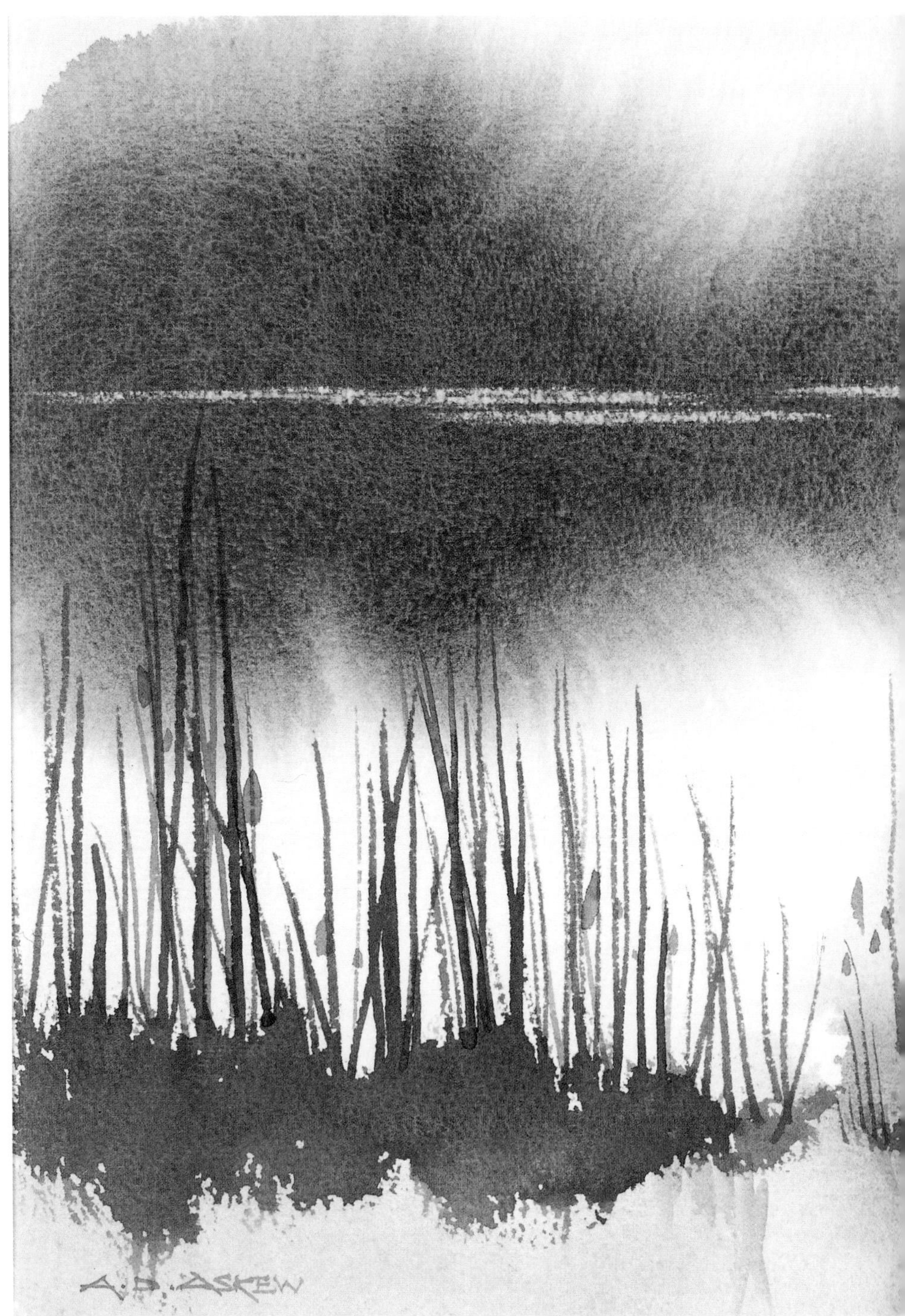

Reed Beds

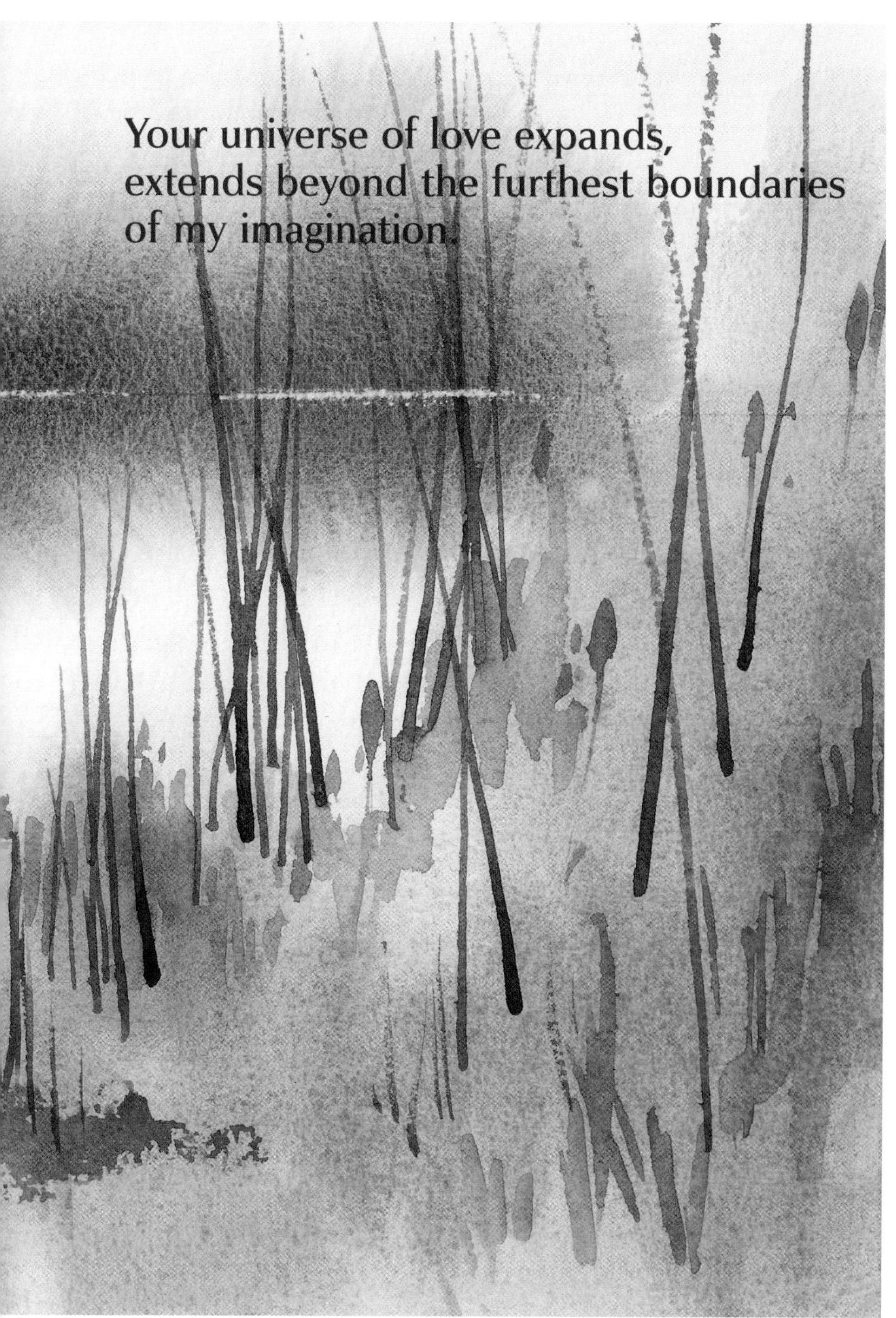

Watercolour

The day on which this took place was a Sabbath,
and so the Jews said to the man who had been healed,
"It is the Sabbath; the law forbids you to carry your mat."
John 5:9-10

There seemed to be little fuss about the man's healing, neither from the crowd nor the man himself. Was there no shout for joy, no hallelujah? It may have been too soon for him to try dancing but surely he made some positive response to what had happened to him? The writer of John's Gospel can be so imaginative and poetic, but here he simply and flatly records the fact that the man walked. That was enough, and maybe the sheer mechanics of walking was all that he could manage at that moment. The joy, the realisation of how it would change his life, would come later. For now, perhaps bewilderment was all he felt as he moved through the crowd, his mat under his arm. He was so overwhelmed by it all that he didn't even ask the name of his healer.

One more thing intrigues me. Faith isn't mentioned. There's no claim that the man had faith in Jesus. At the time he didn't even know who Jesus was, but that didn't prevent Jesus entering the man's life with his love and power. Perhaps there was a seed of faith in the response. He was obedient. He could have stayed there on his mat and never moved. At least he willed himself to try. He did what Jesus asked him to do. "At once the man was cured; he picked up his mat and walked."

And what of the people standing around? Had the miracle gone unnoticed by the crowd? Were people so preoccupied with themselves that they never recognised the one who could have met their own needs too? Missed opportunities rarely return. That's the tragedy of inertia.

There was no immediate reaction from anyone as the man stepped out, until he walked through the town carrying his mat. That did it. First the deafening silence of disapproval, then criticism. There was no wonder at his healing, no rejoicing. It was the Sabbath, the day of rest. The day when no-one was allowed to work. The interpreters of the law had decreed that even carrying a small parcel on the Sabbath was work. Perhaps it was their way of dealing with the unexpected, of taking control of life, an attempt to make it run predictably. The trouble is that in organising life that way, we're in danger of organising out the free movement of the Holy Spirit. God's love doesn't go into neutral on the Sabbath. His forgiveness doesn't have to wait over until Monday morning. It's available now, whatever the time, date or place.

Living by the rules can chain rather than free people. The words of the rule book may become more important than the meaning they hold within them. Jesus knew this and was always prepared to break the rules when human need called for it. "Integrity has no need of rules," said Albert Camus. There's a story about a parrot and a cat. I don't know where it comes from but it holds a truth. The parrot flew freely in the house but it attracted the attention of the cat. The owner said to the parrot, over and over, "When you see the cat, fly to the top of the cupboard." The parrot learned the words. Each time it saw the cat, the parrot repeated the words, "When you see the cat, fly to the top of the cupboard." The trouble was it never understood the real meaning of the words and never flew. The owner came home one day to a pile of green feathers on the carpet. God must laugh at us sometimes – or despair.

It's easier to cling to the letter of the law than live by its spirit. The one is easier than the other. It takes less thought; the decisions are made for us. We see them in every faith, people so intent on observing the rules down to the tiniest details that they lose the big picture. In laying out neat boundaries which can't be crossed, they miss the breathtaking experience of the loving freedom Christ brings. "He is the key that unlocks the door of the prison cell of our own making and sets us free to live in the wide world of God's love and purposes." * He offers each of us the opportunity of getting up from the mat of our inadequacies and the strength to step out into freedom. We can refuse. God forces no-one. Love can't compel. The one thing God can't do is to make someone love him. Some folk are content to live on the edge of the water of the Bethesda pool hoping for a healing that is slow in coming, when they could be drinking the 'living water' that Jesus offers the Samaritan woman at the well (John 4:11 - 14). **

We all fall into the trap one way or another, so let's forget those feelings of superiority. If the rules and customs in our local Christian fellowships seem to exclude people of any sort rather than welcome them, then maybe we should look prayerfully at the rules again. "Dear Lord and Father of mankind, forgive our foolish ways..."

* *Kenneth Pillar,* A Letter to Margaret Pepper, *1987*
** *See* Unexpected Journeys *by Eddie Askew, published by The Leprosy Mission*

Lord, just to be free.
Truly free.
To throw aside the bonds
that tether me,
and step into the freedom
only you can give.
To hear the bird song Adam heard,
to smell the flowers and walk the mountains
in the sunlight of your presence.

You ask what holds me back?
I know – and so do you.
It's me.
I am my own worst enemy,
the obstacle that trips me up,
catches my foot each time I try
to jump the hurdle of my insecurity,
and lands me in the dust.
I see you smile in sympathy and regret –
you wonder why I hesitate so long
to put aside the rules
that hold me in their grip
when all I need to do
is take one infant step towards infinity.

Give me a heart that welcomes,
that rejects rejection and nothing else.
Help me to bridge the ditch
of hasty judgement
and deep-dug prejudice
and share the love and freedom
that you give.

I sometimes wish you'd push me, Lord.
Elbow aside my vacillation,
but freedom means just what it says:
if I am truly free
I'm free to take your freedom or refuse it.
The choice is mine.
So either way I'm free to choose.
And help me, Lord,
to offer this same freedom
to those who break my rules,
who do things in a different way
and challenge me to think again.

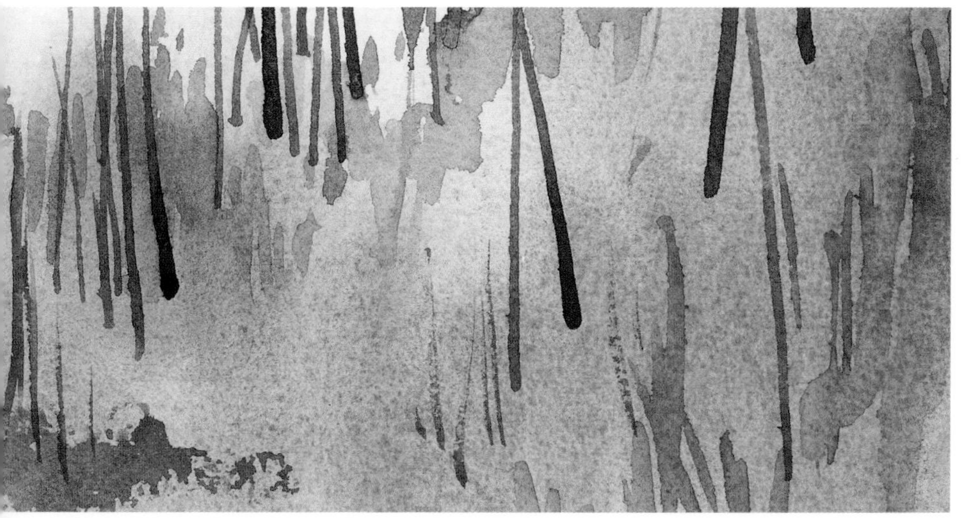

But he replied, "The man who made me well said to me,
"Pick up your mat and walk."
So they asked him,
"Who is this fellow who told you to pick it up and walk?"
The man who was healed had no idea who it was,
for Jesus had slipped away into the crowd that was there.
Later Jesus found him at the temple and said to him,
"See, you are well again. Stop sinning or something worse may
happen to you." The man went away and told the Jews
that it was Jesus who had made him well.

John 5:11-15

The man was brought to earth with a bump. His expanding world held shadows. As he began to find his feet – both metaphorically and literally – he now faced the disapproval of his own community. Was it merely the rude remarks of bystanders or, more likely, the religious authorities? We can't pinpoint exactly where the criticism came from but it had to be answered.

When they asked him why he was carrying his mat, he simply told the truth. He said it was the man who made him well who told him to carry it. That's a great description of Jesus. It's a good start for anyone, however much or little we know him. He's the one who brings truth and healing, and the promise of wholeness to our lives. The one who offers us an experience of the love at the heart of the universe, and sets us on the road to a deeper understanding of God's purposes. I suggest that when we reach the end of our days, if we truly know Jesus as the man who made us well we need little else. It's a description that holds far more than its few words suggest.

But the critics still weren't happy. They rarely are. "Who is this fellow?" they asked. The scorn in those words seems to come to life on the page as I read it. Who was this upstart who put himself above the law of God as they interpreted it. A sad irony. Jesus came to fulfil the law of God, the law of love, to give it its fullest and most sensitive expression, yet his greatest opponents were the most religious. Those who painstakingly and sincerely – and I believe we have to recognise their misguided sincerity – were burying the spirit of God's law under the weight of bureaucracy and legalism. The question they ask is revealing. They weren't interested in who had made the man well, only in who had told him to pick up his bed and walk.

At this point the man didn't know who Jesus was, but he was grateful. He went to the temple to pray, to thank God for his changed life and maybe ask for the strength and courage to cope with the changes it would bring. Could it have been the first time he'd been to worship for 38 years? What an experience. I wonder what memories of childhood and of earlier teaching it brought back to him. He was now whole, no longer barred from the temple for his disability. And that's where Jesus found him. *Found* implies that Jesus went looking for him, not content to leave him as he was. It's all Jesus' initiative. Again I try to picture the meeting. The man was beginning to take in what had happened to him and he meets again the man who made him well. Jesus wants to take the encounter further; the man's healing wasn't yet complete. Jesus speaks to him. "Good things have happened to you," he says, "you're whole and strong and free. Now go out and live your renewed life positively."

Jesus tells him, and us, that if he wants to stay well he has to direct his life towards God, that healing is a dynamic process which goes on throughout life. It offers continual transformation, sometimes comforting, at other times disturbing, but always strengthening and supportive. The choice was left to him, as it is to all of us. And the man goes out and witnesses to Jesus as the one who had made him well.

For many today Jesus remains unrecognised. "He was in the world, and though the world was made through him, the world did not recognise him." (John 1:10) His power and love are at the heart of the universe, and at work in our lives, often unidentified and unacknowledged, offering healing and wholeness, and the promise of new life. The one who made the sick man well can make us whole.

Who are you, Lord?
The theologians seem to know.
They analyse their sacred texts,
define and pigeonhole you,
but I am not convinced they know it all.
There's always more.
Your spirit ranges free,
along your path not theirs.
I've learned that, sometimes painfully,
as adolescent certainties
have been eroded by experience.
How to describe you, Lord?
What name to give that says it all,
that holds the truth of who you are?
You are the many-splendoured Lord
who dances joy into my life,
whose touch gives strength to walk and run,
the one who lights my life with love.

Sometimes I see you clear.
The problem is
that in the blessing of your nearness
I'm tempted to relax
and think I've got it all,
with nothing more to learn.
But when I've used up all my words –
I have a lot of those –
I'm still no nearer to the truth
of who you really are.
There's so much more
beyond the limits of my tiny mind.
Surprises still in store.
And when I've sailed the sea of my perception,
come to the edge
of all I know or think I know,
you come again
in ways I never thought to see,
and I am left in awe and wonder.

And through it all,
my questions
and my search for seeming certainties,
one thing I know and cling to.
You are the one who holds me
in the cradle of your love,
renews me
and gives strength to face another day.
You are the one who makes me well.
Each day.

Sunset on the Estuary

Pastel

Reading - Mark 8:22-26

They came to Bethsaida, and some people brought a blind man and begged Jesus to touch him. He took the blind man by the hand and led him outside the village. When he had spat on the man's eyes and put his hands on him, Jesus asked, "Do you see anything?"

He looked up and said, "I see people; they look like trees walking around."

Once more Jesus put his hands on the man's eyes. Then his eyes were opened, his sight was restored, and he saw everything clearly. Jesus sent him home, saying, "Don't go into the village."

Reading - Mark 10:46-52

Then they came to Jericho. As Jesus and his disciples, together with a large crowd, were leaving the city, a blind man, Bartimaeus (that is, the Son of Timaeus), was sitting by the roadside begging. When he heard that it was Jesus of Nazareth, he began to shout, "Jesus, Son of David, have mercy on me!"

Many rebuked him and told him to be quiet, but he shouted all the more, "Son of David, have mercy on me!"
Jesus stopped and said, "Call him."
So they called to the blind man, "Cheer up! On your feet! He's calling you."
Throwing his cloak aside, he jumped to his feet and came to Jesus.
"What do you want me to do for you?" Jesus asked him.
The blind man said, "Rabbi, I want to see."
"Go," said Jesus, "your faith has healed you." Immediately he received his sight and followed Jesus along the road.

Imagine...

You can't see. Perhaps you can just tell light from dark, or is it only the sun's warmth that distinguishes day from night? You've developed a routine in the darkness. You know the way around your home; the path along the road where you sit and beg, but the larger world confuses, threatens. If you stray off the path you have problems. You can identify some voices, people you know. Others simply come out of nowhere, from any direction, and it's not always easy judging mood when you can't see a face.

As you sit by the roadside you hear shouting in the distance. It gets nearer, louder. People around you are getting excited. Questions pass from one to another. "What's it all about?" "Who's coming?" "Is it somebody special?" "I don't know, I can't see them. Yes, now I can. There's a whole crowd of them." Then the word spreads – "It's Jesus, the new teacher, the healer!" For a moment you sit still, try to stay out of the way of people's feet. Then you think. Jesus the healer? The man you've heard about as you've listened to other people talking. You wonder... Then make up your mind. This is your only chance, he may not come this way again.

You call, but your voice can't be heard in the crowd. You shout louder, wave your arms. Ignore the people around you. It's not the first time you've been sworn at or pushed out of the way. You're an obstacle rather than a person. Then the crowd seems to grow quiet, there's a silence, and one voice calls you. You stand up and unknown hands push you forward. You move towards the sound of the voice and suddenly your hand is caught in other hands. These hands are different. There's a warmth in them. They're strong and firm but they don't compel. They persuade you across the road and you don't hesitate.

Then again you hear the voice. Clear but quieter, the words just meant for you, not for the crowd. "What do you want me to do for you?" he asks. It's personal, you feel his attention is on you, only you. The voice seems to enfold you, gather you into itself. "What do you want?" And in a whisper you reply, "I want to see."

They came to Bethsaida, and some people brought a blind man and begged Jesus to touch him. He took the blind man by the hand and led him outside the village.
Mark 8:22-23

Jesus touched him. Took him by the hand and held him as they walked through the village. Then Jesus put his hand on him, not once but twice. Choosing his words, Mark wants to tell us a story about touch, human contact, intimacy. Touch is important. Some people touch easily, unselfconsciously. Others are more reserved. Either way, people recognise its value. Touch breaks barriers, crosses boundaries. We shake hands, even kiss cheeks, when we first meet someone. It's often the first gesture that brings people together, the touch that turns acquaintances into friends, that transforms friends into lovers. Touch creates trust.

When my small grandchildren need reassurance as we walk in the park, they hold my hand. It's a great feeling of safety. And if they can hold another hand at the same time, they can swing as we walk, trusting even more. People still clasp hands today to seal an agreement as they did in Biblical times, or to end a quarrel. "Shake on it!" we say.

Blindness was common in Jesus' day. Some folk were born blind, many were blind as the result of infection and illness. More stories are recorded in the gospels of Jesus healing the blind than any other illness or disability. It wasn't that Jesus favoured them more than other people but that the gospel writers saw great significance in them. The Bible describes people with little understanding of God's nature as blind. Jesus himself was tough on some of the Pharisees, holier-than-thou people. "Woe unto you, blind guides," he chides them (Matthew 23:16), as people who can't see or who are unwilling to see the truth. (I'd be very uncomfortable if this seemed to imply that blind folk today are less able to see truth than others. That's not so, and I'm sure that wasn't what Jesus meant, and it's certainly not my meaning.)

Bethsaida was a fishing village – the name means a place of fishing – on the northern shore of Galilee, and whatever the blind man was capable of doing, it wouldn't be that. He was too dependent on others and unless he came from a loving and resourceful home, the chances are that he was a beggar. Certainly he needed help. That's why they brought him to Jesus. We don't actually know who brought him – friends or sympathetic bystanders, or even sceptics wanting to test this new healer. Whoever it was they were doing something far more significant than they knew.

Jesus touches the blind man. Takes him by the hand. No longer is he just a voice 'out there' but now they are in close contact. I wonder how it felt to be touched by Jesus. Were his hands still rough, the callused skin a reminder of his days in the building trade as a carpenter? Or had they softened since he'd begun to lead his growing band of followers through the countryside? Was his grip strong or gentle? Warm or cool? Compelling or persuasive? Was it a one-handed touch, or did Jesus envelop the man's hand in both of his? There are so many ways to touch and hold.

There's a chemistry in human touch that brings people closer. Whether it's early teenage innocence, experiencing the thrill of holding someone's hand for the first time, or the gentle comfort of long companionship. To feel another human being, to sense the warmth of another hand, breaches the wall of loneliness and isolation in which some folk live. That's why we take the hand of the patient when we visit someone in hospital, or when we sit beside those who grieve. Touch can say much more than words and can often replace them.

Jesus took him by the *hand*. It wasn't an impersonal touch on the elbow to steer a blind person across a busy road. It was an intimate gesture. Jesus' way of cutting through the formal to the familiar, to bring that personal touch which would go to the heart of need. And when two close friends walk in the dark together, how often they say, "Hold my hand, I can't see." It's good to feel someone close.

Rough hands or smooth?
I think the rough, Lord.
The craftsman's hardened hands,
the hands of one who held a plane
and trued a plank of wood by eye,
met the demands of customers,
and felt the satisfaction
of a job well done.

I'm comforted to think
you knew the world of work,
your muscles tired at the end of day,
and that you felt the trail of sweat
that wet your back in Nazareth.
I'm sure the yokes you made
were smooth and fitted well,
were light as any yoke can be.

And, just in passing, Lord,
may I observe
you said your yoke was easy,
but forgive me when I say
I'm not so sure of that –
I question whether any yoke is weightless –
even yours.

Or is it that I'm not yet used
to carrying it, and maybe
if I were more willing
it would sit a little lighter
on my neck?
But rough or smooth
I'm sure your hand was gentle
as you led him down the road he couldn't see.
A warmth of touch that reassured
and gave him
what he never thought to have.

Lord, take my hand
and hold me in the dark
when I can't see the way ahead.
And if at times I stumble,
as I know I will,
tighten your grip on me
and don't let go.

One thing I know
that in your death and resurrection
new life is grafted on to old
and I'm content
to leave all future growth with you.

Low Tide on the Estuary

Watercolour

He took the blind man by the hand and led him outside the village. When he had spat on the man's eyes and put his hands on him, Jesus asked, "Do you see anything?" He looked up and said, "I see people; they look like trees walking around."

Mark 8:23-24

The wonder of train journeys as a child. Steam trains particularly. Going through a tunnel was a mixture of excitement and apprehension. The train plunged into the darkness with a roar. If we'd left the windows open, the noise would be even louder, and the smell of smoke and the smuts of coal dust would add to the drama. Lights in the compartments where we sat were not always switched on. The train jolted and lurched through unidentified bumps and screeches while we sat in the blackness, waiting. After what seemed hours but was really only seconds, a minute at the most, there would be a gradual lightening of the darkness, a few moments when we began to identify our surroundings and then, suddenly, we were out again into the glorious sunshine. The fields looked greener, the sky bluer, everything brighter – or so it seemed to my young eyes. The experience isn't as impressive with diesels.

Neither would I be impressed by someone spitting in my eye, but in Hebrew culture people believed that saliva had healing properties. We still inherit remnants of that belief. The first thing I do when I cut my finger or burn it on a hot saucepan is to put it in my mouth – my finger, not the saucepan. When someone's been hurt by criticism, we say he's gone away to lick his wounds, and in our childhood most of us suffered that humiliating emergency method of cleaning mud off our face in the park with a handkerchief dampened in mother's mouth!

Jesus was using a method everyone understood and was also continuing the intimacy he began when he grasped the man's hand. He led the man out of the village for privacy but I doubt if they were ever really alone. I know from experience how difficult it is to be alone in an Eastern village. There's always someone following, or peering out from a gateway. Jesus stops and turns to face the blind man. Jesus stands taller – most beggars I've seen in India and elsewhere stoop, their body language non-threatening – then reaches out with a hand each side of the man's face.

"Do you see anything?" Jesus asks. There's a pause as the man blinks, opening and closing his eyes against the sudden brightness of the sun. And in those first moments of sight, the man struggles to make sense of the images he sees. The shapes are strange. First there's Jesus, his face blurred.

Then static trees and bushes, the angular shapes of buildings, and people – more shapes, but moving. It's all alien, confusing, a world he's never seen before. He struggles to relate what he sees now to the way he'd felt things with his hands.

I read a newspaper account by a man who'd been born blind but whose sight had been partially restored by a pioneering method of transplant surgery. He told of the wonder and bewilderment he faced, the difficulty of making sense of what he was seeing. Sometimes, he said, he had to close his eyes to understand what people were saying to him. He found the rapid movements of their lips and eyes and hands too distracting. A 21st century confirmation of the accuracy of the Gospel account.

"Yes, I do see," he says in wonder, "I see people." But finding it impossible so suddenly to take in everything that shouts for his attention he added, "They look like trees walking around." He'd felt trees. Reached up and wondered how high they went. Whenever our younger grandchildren visit, they're hardly through the door before they ask, "May we draw?" And off they rush to my studio. I treasure some of their early drawings. There's a stage at around three years old when children draw people like trees. A scribbled rectangular body, very tall and thin, with arms and legs attached like branches and roots at roughly appropriate places, plus a tiny head on top. (I'm convinced the tiny head comes from the fact that very small children see from the perspective of ground level and the human body looks much bigger than the head from down there!)

The man is beginning to understand and interpret what he sees much as a child would. He's entering a world of wonder. The colours around him, the shimmer of light and shade, the amazing intricacy of a snail shell, the beauty of a bird's feather, are all things that may move him, but all too quickly he will begin to take them for granted, as we all do. And the most exciting thing he will see, once his vision is fully restored, is the face of Jesus. The one who opened his eyes, whose presence brings a brightness and a beauty nothing else can match, but again someone so easy to take for granted.

People like trees walking.
I see them, Lord,
my imagination working overtime.
People like oak trees,
gnarled and scarred by life
but strong, storm-weathered.
People who've faced the world,
absorbed its joys and sorrows
and survived.
Some stand like beeches,
smooth and straight and gracious,
spreading reassurance.
Willows and birches, others,
light and airy as they walk in charm,
scattering leaves of beauty as they go.
The young are saplings,
vulnerable
yet flexible and full of life,
eager for what the future holds.
And just a few I see as pines.
Dry, desiccated folk,
development restricted by their fears
or circumstances out of their control.
The soil in which they've grown
stony and harsh.

Some trees – and folk – grow slowly,
each little gain a measure of achievement.
Others reach out their branches prodigally,
spreading a joy of life
that sets the forest glowing.
But, Lord, I pray
that all may find our roots in you.
That nourished in love,
and fed by grace,
we may grow tall and strong
to face the storms that life will bring.

And then,
I see your cross, a tree itself,
cut down and shaped for death.
And you –
were you stretched out
to fit the cross,
or was the cross stretched out
to fit the arms out-stretched
to hold the world?

One thing I know
that in your death and resurrection
new life is grafted on to old
and I'm content
to leave all future growth with you.
I only ask that pruning
may not hurt too much,
and that the fruit be good to eat.

Once more Jesus put his hands on the man's eyes. Then his eyes were opened, his sight was restored, and he saw everything clearly. Jesus sent him home saying, "Don't go into the village."
Mark 8:25–26

It was eye-opening in more ways than one and must have caused a sensation in the village. The blind man could see. Jesus anticipates the excitement and tells the man to go home. Jesus had touched him twice. Was there an element of resistance in the man, or was Jesus giving him time to adjust to the radical change in his life? Whether he was able to go straight home quietly is an open question. I can't see all those village folk dispersing without making the most of the drama that had just taken place. They'd want to ask questions, talk to the man, talk to Jesus.

The man himself needed a time of quiet to grow into his new experience and calm his emotions. In visual terms he'd been born again. He was a little child, trying to recognise and make sense of the many images bombarding his sight. He would need to relearn so much, to renew and renegotiate his relationships, to put his life on a different level with his family and close contacts. I'm assuming that he – I wish we knew his name – had a family, because Jesus sent him home.

Close contact with Jesus always means rethinking and renewing our relationships. Once he's opened our eyes, he challenges us to renew our vision of the world we live in, and the people with whom we live. In his light we can begin to see ourselves too as we really are, and recognise the masks and cloaks we hide behind, even from ourselves. It's a positive process, sometimes painful but always and ultimately strengthening. It's not to condemn us – I believe we judge ourselves and others more harshly than God does – because the light Jesus throws on us is the light of love. In the 1640s, George Fox, founder of the Society of Friends (Quakers), wrote: "I also saw that there was an ocean of darkness and death; but an infinite ocean of light and love flowed over the ocean of darkness; and in that I saw the infinite love of God." If only we could accept ourselves and each other with just a fraction of the love with which God accepts us, our lives and relationships would be transformed.

It's intriguing that this incident of the blind man's healing is recorded in the gospel immediately after Jesus despairs at his disciples' slowness to understand his teaching (Mark 8:21), and immediately before the disciple Peter identifies Jesus as the Christ (Mark 8:29). Elsewhere, Jesus claims, "I am the light of the world. Whoever follows me will never walk in darkness, but will have the light of life." (John 8:12) Available to all, unsighted or sighted.

In the hectic lifestyle that many of us live, breathing spaces become more and more important. We need time to think and feel, to recognise where we are, what we're doing and where we're going. Not in the sense of continual goal setting which often increases the pressure, but in giving space in our lives for the presence of God to become a felt reality. We can't will it, but we can create a listening space, which God will fill in his own time and in his own way. The busier we are the more we need it. Writing in the 17th century, François de Sale said, "Half an hour's listening (to God) is essential except when you are busy. Then a full hour is needed."

Near the end of his life, Isaac Newton, the scientist who first identified gravity, said that in his life's search he'd done no more than wander on the shoreline of the great ocean of knowledge. He knew there was far more to learn than he could ever grasp. The same is true about our experience of God. It doesn't happen all at once. My experience of him is very different from what it was years ago. That's not because God's changed but because I have. And each change opens my eyes a little more. I just hope that, through it all, the once-blind man was able to keep in his mind a clear picture of the face of Jesus, the man who opened his eyes.

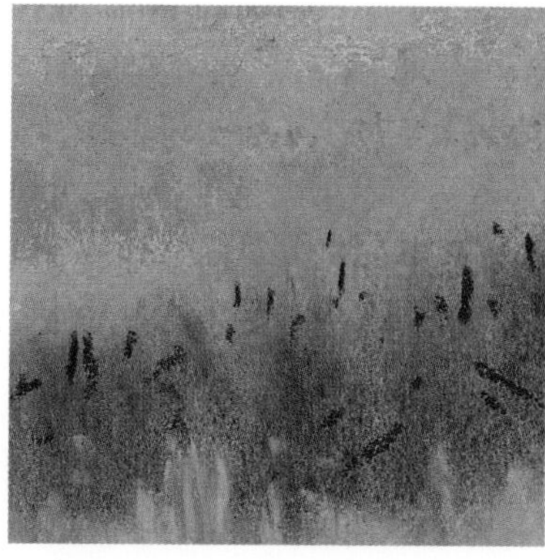

Morning Light on the Estuary

Pastel

Beyond the darkness, Lord,
is light.
Beyond the judgement,
love.
No, not beyond
but in.
There is no darkness that's so deep
your light cannot dispel,
no final judgement that's not tempered
by your love.
And in that light and love
I see myself anew,
not in some cosmic lightning flash,
its harshness blinding in intensity –
I'd not survive the revelation –
but in the gentler kindling
of a tiny candle flame
that tells me all is well,
and that I am accepted as I am
with greater love
than I have ever known
and greater than imagination tells.
My path may lead
through shadowed valley and deep forest –
the mountain tops are rare –
but through them all one thing I know.
I may not be the brightest star
in your great galaxy of saints
but I can shine
with your reflected light
and that's enough
to keep me going
for today.

"What do you want me to do for you?" Jesus asked him.
Mark 10:51

Bartimaeus was a different character. He didn't wait for someone to lead him gently to Jesus. His blindness hadn't tamed him. He was still a personality to be reckoned with. Surrounded by the crowd, he shouts, kicks up a fuss. Those around him are annoyed. "Shut up," they growl, "Who do you think you are?" He shouts again. "Ignore him," cries the crowd, "He's only a beggar." He's hemmed in. He can't be seen and the opportunity will never come again. This is his only chance. He shouts louder, desperately. There's no mistaking him now. He will be heard!

Unlike the other blind man, Bartimaeus is named. He's the son of Timaeus. We don't know who his father Timaeus was or what he did, but being named makes Bartimaeus special, although he's still a blind beggar. He was sitting at the roadside near one of the city gates. Jericho was an ancient city even in Jesus' time. It was an important city too, the focus of several trade routes, and the main roads and gates through its protective walls were always busy. Travellers moved in and out with their trade goods, pilgrims passed through on their way to Jerusalem, 15 miles away, and the city gate was the traditional place where traders made deals and agreed contracts. A place full of interest and movement.

It was a city of palm trees, a beautiful city for those who could see, but for blind Bartimaeus it was simply a place to beg. He must have been a nuisance sitting by the roadside, an obstacle to people walking by, someone to fall over and curse. His hand was always stretched out, his cry for charity strident. He needed a thick skin and persistence if he was to survive, and judging by the noise he made to attract Jesus' attention, he had all that. It was a hard life.

Jesus too was surrounded by the crowd. Mark's writing tells us he and his followers were leaving the city, Luke's informs us that they were entering (Luke 18:35). Let's not quibble or make too much of that. Eye-witness accounts often differ, and details get altered as stories are handed down. The essentials are the same. Bartimaeus suddenly wakes up to Jesus' presence. Maybe he'd heard the name in the conversations going on around him, or perhaps he'd simply asked someone nearby as the crowd's excitement grew. He certainly knew who Jesus was; he called him "Son of David", a clear description of the Messiah they were waiting for. He calls again. Jesus stops, looks around, then calls him over. Bartimaeus leaps to his feet and drops his cloak. No, not drops, throws it aside. However threadbare that cloak, it would have been precious to him. A cloak to keep him warm against the cold nights. Days were warm in Jericho but nights could be cold down in the Jordan valley. He allows nothing to get in the way of his chance to meet Jesus.

Then comes Jesus' question. Jesus asked a lot of questions of the people he met, and often the questions were deeper than they first appeared. He'd asked the paralysed man at Bethesda's pool, "Do you want to get well?" Now he asks, "What do you want me to do for you?" Jesus' question seems to have a life of its own. It leaps off the page, directs itself at me. It echoes down the centuries into my life and yours. A question Jesus asks today as he walks the road or stands looking through the busy crowds. We can shrug and turn away, pretend we haven't heard it. It's up to us. We can respond without much effort as the other blind man did. We may think that opening up just a part of our lives and asking for some small blessing is enough. Or we can take a deep breath and ask for the one thing that will change us forever.

Would Bartimaeus simply ask for money as he did at the roadside every day, or would he ask for more? There was no hesitation. He knew Jesus was special and he had the faith to believe that Jesus could heal him. This was his crisis point. At that moment his whole world stood still; he knew what he wanted more than anything else. "Teacher," he replied, "I want to see." And his eyes were opened.

What do I want, Lord?
You really want to know?
Sight, understanding,
and the strength
your never-failing presence promises.
Courage and persistence
to live as you would have me live.
Persistence, did I say?
That's hard,
I make an effort for a day or two
but then my battery runs down
and once again the darkness threatens me.
And courage?
Yes, the nerve to go on trusting
when things don't happen
at the speed of light.
The bloody-mindedness –
forgive the phrase,
it really does describe the state of mind –
that keeps me going
when all the world seems bent
on riding roughshod over me
and I am left
behind the uncaring crowd.
I call your name
but things get in the way.
Times when my voice is overlaid
by circumstance beyond control,
and I'm not always sure you're listening.
I'm tempted then to curl up
in the cloak of my defensiveness
and turn away.
But something deep inside urges me on,
your spirit, Lord, already there.
I call again, a little louder,
but not so loud to cause
the neighbours to complain,
just loud enough to make you turn.
And when I hear you asking yet again
what do I want?
The answer's clear.
It's you.

Immediately he received his sight and followed Jesus along the road.

Mark 10:52

It's interesting to compare Bartimaeus with the other, unnamed, blind man. The latter seemed to take no initiative. He was a person who went with the flow, to whom things simply happened. Other people led him to Jesus and spoke for him. There was no mention of faith, and the healing was more gradual, perhaps because his slower personality needed time to accept and adjust to what was happening in his life. Bartimaeus was extrovert, persistent, almost aggressive in his determination to get to Jesus. Nothing could be allowed to stand in his way. He abandoned his cloak, and presumably his mat, his begging bowl and anything else he may have had with him. It was all thrown aside. Whatever he'd heard about Jesus created the faith to believe that Jesus could help him. He had only one thought: he was totally committed.

After Jesus opens Bartimaeus' eyes he tells him to go – as he told the first man. But again Bartimaeus is different. The other man, the one with the quieter personality, does just what he's told to do and disappears from the story, but for Bartimaeus it wasn't over. There were times when Jesus confronted people with an open challenge to follow him. That's how he called his first disciples, Peter and Andrew, James and John, as they were fishing by the lakeside. "Come," he'd said, "Follow me." Now he tells Bartimaeus to go.

As always, I try to hear Jesus' tone of voice. I don't believe the words were a sharp command, "Go away", but more gentle words that implied that the meeting between them was over. More a "You can go now." Bartimaeus had been healed, he was free to go wherever he chose.

continued overleaf

I see Bartimaeus standing still, looking at Jesus. He turns his head slowly, taking in the people, the trees, the buildings. Then he looks down the road. A road he'd known well, although this was the first time he'd seen it with his eyes. It led back to the known, to his past life. He looks again at Jesus, then at the road ahead. It left the city gates behind and led into the unknown. There would be no certainty on that road, but he would travel with the one who'd opened his eyes. The decision is made. He follows Jesus. But there's a slight ambiguity about the phrase. It could mean that he just followed for a short time to say thank you, but most commentators suggest that he became a disciple. A few go so far as to suggest that the reason we're given Bartimaeus' name is because he became a well-known personality among early Christians. It may seem a great transformation from beggar to disciple but that, after all, is what Jesus offers to each one of us the moment we are ready to throw off all that holds us back. He'll renew our vision, open the door to the freedom that he can give. All he asks is that we follow him along the road.

Lord,
I'm just a bit confused.
To come or go?
I stand with Bartimaeus
in the middle of the road.
A choice to make,
to go with you
or stay with what I know?
The strong wind of your presence
blows through my life
and shakes the leaves of my security.
It would be easier to stay,
to hold to what I know –
or think I know, there is a difference, Lord –
but something, someone,
draws me out and on.

You don't insist,
you leave me free to choose
to stay with you or go,
but there's a strange compulsion
in the freedom that you give.
A magnetism that I cannot break,
that draws me on and in.
I'm free to turn my back,
and change my new-found riches
back to rags.
Say "Thank you, but no thanks."
It's up to me.

But, Lord, I cannot let you go.
I know you are the one who opens eyes,
whose hands hold healing.
And if the price for that
is taking to the road without a map,
I'll take the road.
And one day,
looking back along the way I've travelled,
I'll realise there was a plan
that marked the road
you walked with me.

Under the Trees, South Africa

Part Three

There's a place for us

Watercolour

Reading - Mark 1:35-45

Very early in the morning, while it was still dark, Jesus got up, left the house and went off to a solitary place, where he prayed. Simon and his companions went to look for him, and when they found him, they exclaimed: "Everyone is looking for you!"

Jesus replied, "Let us go somewhere else – to the nearby villages – so that I can preach there also. That is why I have come." So he travelled throughout Galilee, preaching in their synagogues and driving out demons.

A man with leprosy came to him and begged him on his knees, "If you are willing, you can make me clean."
Filled with compassion, Jesus reached out his hand and touched the man. "I am willing," he said, "Be clean!" Immediately the leprosy left him and he was cured.

Jesus sent him away at once with a strong warning: "See that you don't tell this to anyone. But go, show yourself to the priest and offer the sacrifices that Moses commanded for your cleansing, as a testimony to them." Instead he went out and began to talk freely, spreading the news. As a result, Jesus could no longer enter a town openly but stayed outside in lonely places. Yet the people still came to him from everywhere.

Imagine...

Peter wakes to the murmur of people on the road outside the house. For a moment he's not sure where he is. He lies quietly, and stretches. Then he remembers the excitement of the night before. So many people healed. They'd been so persistent, reluctant to go away. Now they're back. At this early hour. There's knocking at the courtyard gate and voices clamouring for Jesus. Peter gets up. He goes over to where Jesus was sleeping, but he's not there. The sleeping mat's unoccupied, and his robe's missing. He looks around and, as he realises Jesus isn't in the house, he has a moment of panic. He's gone. Jesus often goes out on his own in the early morning, but surely not today, not after last night. He's needed here, now.

There's more noise from outside, more shouting, and Peter doesn't know how to deal with the folk gathering. What to do? He calls one of the others, you, and together you ease open the gate and slip through. The gate closes behind you. The crowd presses in, shouting. People catch at your hands and clothes, but with a muttered explanation you shoulder your way through, Peter using his fisherman's strength. A few people follow with questions, but they soon turn back. It's Jesus they want. You're not sure where he's gone but you head uphill, following the rough path that generations of animal and human feet have worn in the earth.

Golden light is flooding over the hills to the east. It trickles, then pours over the crest of the Golan Heights and down the hillside, first gliding over the rough pasture, then taking in the lower cultivated fields. The trees stretch long shadows towards you and, as you climb higher, the noise of the crowd is subdued. You're not quite sure where you're going but you know that Jesus likes quiet places in the hills. You look around, up to the crest where early morning sheep crop the grass, then down to the lake-shore. The water's still, its surface sparkling with sunshine. In the distance a few fishing boats are labouring their way back with the night's catch. There's no wind and rowing would be hard work, but for a moment Peter wishes he was with them.

The path is steep. You pause, take a deep breath and look around. Then you see Jesus in the distance. A small figure wrapped in his cloak, sitting on the ground in the shelter of a large rock. He's slipped off his sandals,

continued overleaf

and sits with his arms round his knees, looking out over the water. Never one to wait, Peter pants up the last few yards and stands in front of him, hands on hips, breathing heavily. "Teacher," he gasps, "they want you down there." Jesus looks at Peter, then looks away. He's silent for a moment. Then he speaks. "No, Peter," he answers, "there are others who need me too. We can't just stay here."

Peter looks at Jesus, then down the hill to the houses. "But..." He checks, then moves from one foot to the other, trying to understand. Trying to balance the persistent demands of the people in Capernaum with the needs of unseen people further away. It's hard for him to fathom.

"Everyone is looking for you!"

Mark 1:37

It was a startling way for Jesus to begin his public life. A riveting sermon (when did I last hear one of those?) and the sensational healing of a man with mental illness. The news spread rapidly. When Sabbath restrictions ended after sunset, an excited crowd gathered around the house. Jesus and his small group of companions were besieged.

Soon it would be dark, usually a time to relax over supper and talk about the day, but not this evening. The food got cold as more people came and Jesus walked among them, listening and talking, reassuring and healing. Finally, the courtyard gate was closed and barred, the people outside dispersing reluctantly. Exhausted, Jesus and the disciples ate a quick supper, climbed the stairs to the flat roof and collapsed on to their beds. Some fell asleep immediately, others lay staring into the night sky, replaying in their minds all that had happened that day. It was only a short time since Simon Peter and Andrew, James and John had left their fishing boats and followed Jesus. Now they had more questions than answers churning around in their minds. What were they getting into? Who was this teacher they'd left home for and followed so eagerly? Where did his power come from? Where was he leading them? Questions still relevant 2,000 years later. They were entering a new world, an uncertain future, with a mixture of excitement, wonder and apprehension. Far different from the life they'd known as fishermen.

And what of Jesus? We know nothing of his own thoughts, even struggles, as he lay there in the dark, seeking to understand and accept the healing power God was directing through him. I can't believe that he ever took it for granted. The power was his through committed and sustained prayer.

At daybreak, people were gathering again, but when Peter went to wake Jesus all he found was an empty sleeping mat. Jesus had slipped quietly away without anyone hearing. Was there a back gate, or had he climbed over the courtyard wall? Whatever it was, he needed time to think and pray. Time just to be alone.

Alone? No, not alone. There was this loving presence, unseen but close, the presence he addressed as *Abba*, father. In passing, I can only believe that Joseph the carpenter must have been a very loving parent for Jesus to identify God as *father*. Early experiences greatly influence our later understanding of life and our relationships with other people.

Sitting up on the hillside above Capernaum Jesus watched the sun rise, felt its warmth, heard the early bird song, looked out over the water. A time of beauty and peace, a time when the heartbeat slows, breathing deepens, and the open spaces welcome and absorb you. Jesus had found a quiet moment and the space he needed to open himself to the presence of God.

But not for long. Disciples were gasping up the hill, calling. I remember a morning like that in Galilee. I was co-leading a Holy Land pilgrimage of about 30 people, a fairly demanding occupation. One morning I got up early, walked across the road from the hotel and sat on the beach overlooking the lake. There was no-one about except the birds. Gulls, persistent sparrows, a pied kingfisher making its first patrol of the day. It was beautiful, quiet, relaxing, but soon I had to move. There was a group to lead, preparations to be made, work to be done.

Peter stands, breathing heavily, looking down on Jesus. "They want you," he said, nodding at the houses down below. There was a pause as Jesus looks out over the lake, then looks at him. Jesus answered, "No," quietly but firmly. "We've been here long enough, it's time to move on." It would have been easy, and must have been tempting, to stay. A crowd at your feet, the satisfaction of helping people and, dare I say it, the ego-trip of so many people wanting what you could give. Yet it would have been a trap to allow himself to sink into a warm bath of admiration. It can be hard to turn away, to leave the small successes behind and move out into the unknown, but that's what Jesus chose to do.

It created a dilemma, one I'm sure the disciples felt. There *were* more people needing help down in Capernaum, but immediate demands can sometimes blind us to longer-term opportunities. The need wasn't limited to Capernaum. It was widespread. Feelings, insights, commonsense and the expectations of other people aren't always easy to reconcile. It needs time, space and prayer. And if Jesus needed that, then so do we. It's hard to find those breathing spaces in our busy lifestyles but the more we fill up our time with activity, however well-meaning, the more difficult it gets to find the space in which good decisions can be made.

By our endless and often enthusiastic activity we can crowd out the one in whose name we claim to be working. We may have to face criticism and misunderstanding when we say "No", or when we move on, but it may be the right thing to do. We're not told how the crowd felt, standing outside the house waiting for Jesus to reappear, or how Peter dealt with it. He was at the beginning of a steep learning curve with Jesus. Aren't we all?

Forgive me, Lord, for saying it,
but you're so unpredictable.
It would be great
if I could know exactly
when and where
I could make contact.
But sometimes when I look for you
there's just an empty space
where I expected you to be.
Living with you
can be a game of hide and seek.
I count to ten,
then look for you behind each bush –
none burning, Lord –
but you're not there.
I'd like to feel you near,
to know that you're around
and waiting for my every call.
But that's not how it works for me.
Times when the line seems down,
the service interrupted,
no reassuring word about the engineer.
Even a recorded message
would be comforting,
asking me to leave a number
and saying you'll get back to me
at a more convenient time.
Not really satisfactory, Lord,
but better than the silence.
And yet I know you're there,
and with me always,
just as you said
and as my past experience tells me.
That's why I find it hard to understand,
that when I really need your voice,
your hand to guide me as I face today,
I find I'm out of touch.
My cries for help
come bouncing back,
each echo weaker than the one before.

Yet, in the final echo,
I can faintly hear
the whisper of your voice
saying "I'm still here.
It's simply that you need
some space to grow,
to find the strength
to make your own decisions."
Yes, Lord, I hear,
and though I may not like the message,
I agree.
I have some growing up to do.

Quiet Afternoon, Abydos, Egypt

And so I ask you Lord,
to help me see
the glory of your image
in the folk I meet today
and every day.

Watercolour

A man with leprosy came to him and begged him on his knees, "If you are willing, you can make me clean."

Mark 1:40

It's the word *clean* that gets under my skin. Most sick people simply want to get well. To be normal. This man wanted to be clean. It worries me that someone ill and anxious about his health should believe that he was unclean; that there was a moral burden attached to his illness. But that was the belief of his day. The religious authorities, the people with knowledge and power, had said so.

He was *unclean*; not with the honourable dirt of a day's work in the fields, easily washed away, but with a deeper ritual uncleanness placed on him by the priests. It built a wall between him and his community, a wall no-one was allowed to climb. Even the synagogue, his place of worship, was closed to him.

Once again we know little about the man. We're not told his name, his age, or where he came from. Truthfully, we can't even be sure that he was suffering from what we would diagnose today as leprosy. The word the Bible uses, *tsara'at*, covered a wide range of disfiguring skin diseases, of which today's leprosy was just one. Assuming that the man had leprosy, what did Jesus see? In the early stage of the illness, there's little to see. A few discoloured patches of skin, easily covered by clothing. But when we read Dr. Luke's account he says the man was "covered with leprosy". (Luke 5:12) This suggests he had suffered for years, that the illness was advanced, and the man disfigured and disabled.

There's beauty and dignity in the human body – think of its creator – and it's a tragedy when it's disfigured by illness. Jesus saw a man made in the image of God, an image now broken by suffering and rejection. Yet whatever the outward condition, however unappealing the appearance, God's likeness was present in him and is in all of us. It may be hidden, it may struggle in vain to get out from under layers of distortion, but deep down it's part of our nature. The image of God in every cell, chromosome and gene of our being. "We are God's workmanship," writes St. Paul. (Ephesians 2:10) The presence of God in our lives makes the ordinary extraordinary, and the extraordinary ordinary. The poet, Gerard Manley Hopkins wrote, "The world is charged with the grandeur of God."* The most routine of our activities can glow with God's glory if we do

* *From the poem God's Grandeur*

them for him, and the presence of his Spirit in our lives becomes a daily reality, the norm which I suggest he intended in the beginning. I have a feeling that it's ugliness that's only skin-deep, not beauty.

That wasn't the way the community saw the leprosy sufferer. It had rejected him. It had torn out the roots of his life and thrown him on the scrapheap. Perhaps too his perceived uncleanness was a projection of the community's own feelings, laying on him their own inadequacies and fears. How often we reject what we fear in ourselves, without ever recognising it.

I wonder how the man saw himself. So much of our identity is attached to where we live and what we do. How quickly we ask a new acquaintance, "Where do you come from? What do you do?" He belonged nowhere, he was rootless and dispossessed. But worse – the man felt himself rejected by God, punished for some unknown, unnamed sin. This is how many leprosy sufferers see themselves today, and why I am unhappy when I hear Christian preachers speak about "the leprosy of sin". It's a tempting analogy, particularly when we acknowledge Jesus' power over both, but to suggest even indirectly that the two are related is less than helpful. Perhaps too the man had rejected himself. Our self-image is important, and that includes the way we look. Remember how you felt as a teenager with a spot on your nose? I've known seriously disabled patients in India who reject their own injured limbs. Patients who refuse to take the slightest precaution to prevent further damage because "There's no feeling in this hand. It doesn't feel like mine." It's easy to blame oneself for the situation. "It must be my fault." And for people like that, acceptance is more important than pills.

He was imprisoned in his condition but he found the strength to break the rules and come to Jesus. Even approaching Jesus was unlawful. The 'uncleanness' could be passed on to anyone with whom he came into contact but he was making a last ditch effort to regain the humanity he had so nearly lost. It was also a tremendous leap of faith to believe that Jesus could heal and restore him.

And Jesus reached out to him across the boundaries set by a legalistic and defensive society which sacrificed compassion to protect its own position. A message relevant today.

Have patience, Lord,
I'm in a serious bout of introspection
and need to talk it through with you.
When I look into my life with honesty
– as much as I can bear, that is –
I realise how easily
I sit in judgement
and how enjoyable the process feels.
So easy to identify
another person's failings
and, their fault or not,
I love to throw the stones of prejudice
across the surface of their life
and count how many times they bounce.

Yet who am I to judge them anyway?
Where do I find the arrogance
to condemn whom you accept?
To show dislike for those you love?
To spurn the contact
that might let me see
the beauty underneath the skin.

Loving my neighbour
– and incidentally
I've never really wondered
whether he finds loving me
a problem too –
might be a little easier
if I recognised your presence in his life.
And so I ask you Lord,
to help me see
the glory of your image
in the folk I meet today and every day.
And if I find it difficult to see,
help me to look more closely
with the same compassion
that you use on me.
And may that seed of love
transform my life
as well as theirs.

Filled with compassion, Jesus reached out his hand and touched the man. "I am willing," he said. "Be clean!" Immediately the leprosy left him and he was cured.
Mark 1:41-42

Immediately. There's an urgency about this first chapter of Mark's gospel. There's excitement, tension, a breathlessness in it. Look through it and note the number of times he uses the words *at once* or *immediately*. Things are happening which have never happened before; things that will change the world. This is one of them.

The man is on his knees, arms outstretched, his eyes on Jesus, watching and waiting. Jesus reacts with compassion. We've devalued that word. Today, *compassion* suggests sympathy, pity. They're good things to feel, but they're passive, not very strong. The word is really two words joined together – *com* and *passion*. With passion; and passion meant *suffering*. We speak of Christ's passion, his suffering on the cross. That's powerful stuff. It's also linked to the Greek word meaning *guts* – the heart and stomach, which were thought to be the focus of human emotion. After all, when we're faced with a crisis, something threatening, we feel sick, our stomachs churn, we're "moved to the depth of our being".* Jesus enters the man's life, feels his pain, identifies with his loneliness and rejection – a hint of the rejection and pain which Jesus himself was to face later.

The New English Bible perhaps gets nearer to the original feel, translating the word *compassion* as *warm indignation*. Jesus is indignant, even angry, not at the man for approaching him, but at the society which has added to the man's suffering by its judgement and expulsion. When we're faced with the deprivation and misery of so many of the world's people today anger at the injustice might be a more appropriate emotion than sympathy. Properly channelled, anger gets things done. And while we're in this mood, I wonder who we reject, who do we keep on the edge of our communities? How do we show the active love Jesus calls us to show?

Jesus reached out and touched him. Again, what sort of touch? A light movement of the hand, or could it have been a hug, arms round his shoulders, faces near? Whichever, it was an action the man wouldn't have expected. No-one touched an 'unclean' leprosy sufferer. How did the disciples react? I would love to have seen their faces. Were they excited,

* *From* Images of Jesus by Anselm Gruen, *published by Continuum 2001*

apprehensive, horrified? Were they standing close to Jesus or had they moved back a little to escape contamination? When crises come, do we stand firmly alongside Jesus or do we too step smartly back?

In an instant Jesus creates a bond between him and the sick man, and the man is transformed. Immediately. The urgency is there, his suffering so all-embracing that nothing can be allowed to get in the way. He could have been healed physically without the touch but, for a man starved of human contact, a touch was what he needed most. One intimate gesture from Jesus broke down the wall of rejection which had hemmed the man in, and resolved the conflict within the man himself.

Jesus says, "Be clean!" This doesn't imply that Jesus accepted the attitude of the community – all he'd done showed the opposite. He's simply using language the man would understand. Jesus offers him the chance to rid himself of the resentments, the self-hatred, all that overlaid his humanity. The man stands up, his back straight, a new creation. "The glory of God", said the Greek theologian, Irenaeus, 1,900 years ago, "is man fully alive." Jesus' touch is the one thing that can bring us alive; that can resolve the conflicts within our own personalities. It may not always happen with the immediacy it did here, but through Jesus' eyes we begin to see ourselves as we really are and the wonder of what we can become. Then we can take the first step on the road to wholeness which he offers to each one of us.

Lord, you can make me whole.
I know you can.
I know you will.
I feel your spirit
blowing through my life,
moving the rubbish of the years.
Dusty regrets,
long-treasured hurts, so lovingly retained,
the dried and crumbling leaves
of heaped resentments hoarded still.
Piled high, they work their poison,
hinder my healing,
and stunt the growth that could be mine.

Stretch out your hand, Lord,
just one brief touch will do
– although a hug would really make my day –
to sweep away the fallen leaves
that clog the ground between us.
I realise it may take time,
perhaps the urgency is not for me,
your healing is a work of grace,
your grace,
my restoration
something only you can give.
I wait Lord, on my knees,
to hear you say, "I will."

Jesus sent him away at once with a strong warning:
"See that you don't tell this to anyone."

Mark 1:43-44

We can't pin Jesus down. No label fits. His words and actions are unpredictable. We can't tame him. Life would be safer and less surprising if we could. Many people try, but I see Jesus smiling ruefully at our attempts to fit him into the comfortable world we create for ourselves. Theology is meant to help us understand more of God's nature, but we sometimes use it to keep him in a box and to control the way people think about him. It isn't meant to do that. We can't control him and it's a waste of time to attempt it. But, taken together, the apparent contradictions in his behaviour add up to a clear and consistent witness to the truth. One minute Jesus is a rebel – an image I treasure and tend to follow rather more than I should – but the next moment he shows deep respect for the Jewish Law. His apparent breaking of the rules is actually cutting through the superficial to the core of God's law – which is to love him and love our neighbour. Any rule that obstructs that is faulty, whatever texts we use to justify it.

In his dealing with the leprosy sufferer, Jesus was breaking strong prohibitions. The man was 'unclean' and in touching him Jesus was taking the uncleanness on himself. It was no accident. Jesus embraced it deliberately to show that the judgement which had rejected the sick man was human and flawed. Overturning convention, "breaking the tyranny of normality" as someone memorably put it, refusing to do what was expected. Jesus recognised both the humanity and the divine image in the man. An image and humanity that Jesus shared. It may be hard to recognise God's image in some people we meet but it's there, deep down. We need to be reminded, whether for our own sake, or for the way we see others, that we are all made only "a little lower than the angels." (Psalm 8:5)

Compassion ruled. Would that we could re-examine our rules and expectations from the same viewpoint, and embrace and accept the people we exclude. When Jesus described the coming kingdom in his story of the great banquet (Luke 14:15-23), it was the poor and disabled, the blind and lame who were welcomed; the rough-sleepers and the drop-outs. The respectable and law-abiding lost out.

Going back to this incident, why did Jesus instruct the man to tell no-one what had happened? We don't know, we're not told. Some suggest that

Jesus didn't wish to be known simply as a miracle healer – although he didn't give the same instruction to other people he healed. Maybe it was because leprosy was seen as different and special – only God was believed to have the power to heal leprosy. And maybe, just maybe, Jesus is continuing to be a rebel. In touching the man Jesus had made himself 'unclean'. If people got to know, it might have hindered Jesus' movements and contacts. Would people still have crowded around him? Maybe it was better that people didn't know. It would certainly have provoked the authorities.

Yet Jesus' breaking of the Jewish Law is balanced by a respect for the truth that lay beneath the Law. "Go," he said to the man, "show yourself to the priest."

Lord, rebellion comes quite easily to me.
I'm always ready to protest,
to question "why?"
and break the rules that others make,
shrug off constraints, go my own way
and use my freedom any way I wish.
And yet it's different
when it comes to my own rules.
The rules I make and treasure
are the rules that keep at bay
the folk who make demands on me,
disrupt the comfortable journey of my faith
with calls for help.

I have enough to do
without the burden of other peoples' problems
and flashes of reality breaking in.
Just you and me along the road,
that's what I like,
an easy road where every milestone's clear
to read and understand,
not hidden by the beggars on the way.
A road where all the obstacles
– the puddles and the rocks – are well defined
and I've no need to muddle through the mire
or bruise my shins
on the sharp corners of commitment
any harder than I'm comfortable with.

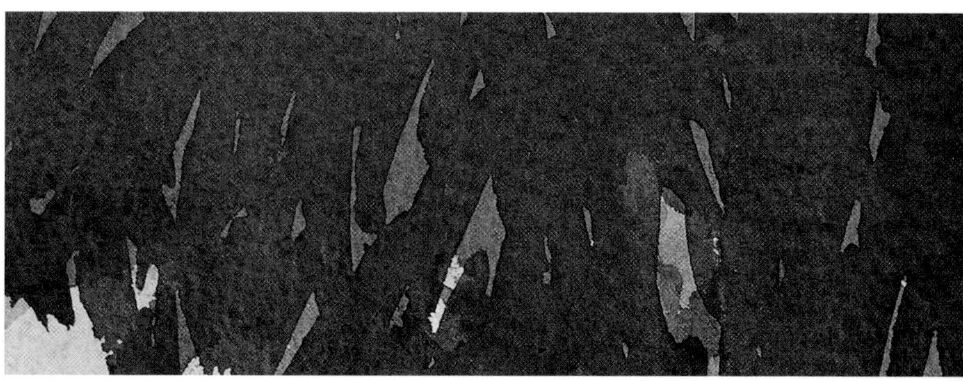

That would be fine,
but that's not how you travel.
You are the Way,
and I accept you know full well
where you are heading,
but in your presence I can feel embarrassed
by the company you keep.
The path gets crowded by the sort of folk
I never thought to travel with.

And still you lead me on
and in your eyes
the love and understanding that I lack
shines bright for vulnerable travellers on the way.
And suddenly I realise – what took so very long? –
that I am one with them,
no different,
in need of all the help that I can get.

I've many miles to go
and much to learn.
Stay close.

And still you lead me on
and in your eyes
the love and understanding that I lack
shines bright for vulnerable travellers
on the way.

Good Drying Weather, Abydos, Egypt

Watercolour

"But go, show yourself to the priest and offer the sacrifices that Moses commanded for your cleansing, as a testimony to them."
Mark 1:44

In *West Side Story*, a musical by Leonard Bernstein, based loosely on the story of Romeo and Juliet, the tragic lovers sing, "There's a place for us, somewhere a place for us" – a place where they would be accepted and loved for who they really were. They never found it. They were held apart by the prejudices of their different communities. But there was a place for the man with leprosy. He'd given up all hope of regaining it until he found new life in Jesus.

Jesus encourages him to return to God in gratitude, and to deepen his relationship with him. The Lebanese poet, Kahlil Gibran, writes in his book *The Prophet*, "You pray in your distress and in your need: would that you might pray also in the fulness of your joy and in your days of abundance." Something we might all learn to do. I'm much quicker to pray for help when I need it than I am to say thank you when it comes.

Jesus the rebel turns back to the teaching of the law. Without respect for the traditions, the man he has healed will not be welcomed back into his community. So he sends him back to the priest, to make the sacrifices the law expected. He points the man back to God. This is great, although I suspect there's a moment of irony here.

When the man's illness first became noticeable, he had to go to the priest for diagnosis, and it was the priest, acting on behalf of the community, who had pronounced him unclean and expelled him. Now, whether it was the same priest or another – probably another because years must have elapsed between the beginning and end of the illness – it was a priest who had to recognise the cure, and restore him to his rightful place in society. I only hope that once the priest had got over his first moments of doubt and disbelief he accepted the man gladly.

In offering the sacrifices, the man's healing is publicly recognised and confirmed, and he is accepted into the heart of the community – the Temple in Jerusalem. That's where sacrifices were offered. As comprehensively as he was shunned, so now he is reaffirmed and reintegrated into his spiritual home. Jesus the healer recognises and emphasises the unity of body, mind and spirit. No healing is complete without it, a truth health workers are increasingly recognising today.

I wonder how quickly the man was able to accept himself again. How soon was he able to deal with his self-rejection and learn to value and love what he had become? And what he's been all the time. Jesus opened a door to new life, but the man had to step through it to find his real self. This would have been an essential part of his healing, as it is of ours. We sometimes miss the truth that in trying to love our neighbour as part of our living faith we must first, or at least at the same time, learn to love and accept ourselves. Again, Kahlil Gibran has an insight. "Your neighbour," he says, "is your other self dwelling behind a wall." And we often build the wall ourselves.

Another part of this healing process is learning the glorious truth that God loves each one of us, whatever our condition. There are many who yearn for a place in a community, a Christian community. They are already on the fringe but hold back from a deeper commitment because they feel inadequate. "I'm not good enough, I'm not worthy." True – a week's experience in any Christian community would tell them that none of us is good enough. The great news is that it doesn't matter. It may be important to you but it doesn't matter to God. He loves us now for what we are, there is no small print and there are no qualifying clauses. God loves with an all-embracing, all-consuming love, which sweeps us into his healing arms the moment we let go of the dis-ease that holds us back. There is a place for each one of us.

Thanks be to God.

Lord, I'm overwhelmed.
It's just too much for me to understand.
Why you,
creator of the galaxies,
the power that spins the planets,
weaves the stars into your tapestry of love
can still have time for me.
I would have thought the universe
would be enough for you.

It's easier to turn it round
and make a case for me to do the work.
Not of the universe
but at the very least to struggle,
strive to make myself a little less unworthy,
a little more acceptable to you.
To contribute some effort to the task myself
would make me feel deserving of your love,
until I realise it can't be done.
However hard I try, I fail.

But that's not how it works.
However much I try to please,
to build up 'Brownie points',
I have no strength, no virtue
that can justify myself to you.
But this I know –
although I hardly dare to state the fact –
you love me as I am,
and have done since before the world began
and will beyond its end.
I'm caught up in your universe of love,
expanding far beyond belief or measurement.
A love that fills my life,
surrounds and saturates,
that guards and guides my every step.
A love that holds me safe,
not from *but* in *life's dangers*
and keeps me close.

Lord, as I said before,
I'm overwhelmed but reassured.
You love me as I am.
It's all too much for me
yet something deep within me
says it is enough.
I do not need to understand,
simply accept.

Jesus could no longer enter a town openly but stayed outside in lonely places. Yet the people still came to him from everywhere.

Mark 1:45

I wonder if Jesus really expected the man he'd healed to stay quiet? How could he? He'd just experienced the most momentous and impossible event in his life. He was bubbling with excitement, needing to share, to tell others, to shout it from the housetops. He was sharing the joy and wonder of the Psalmist who sang, "You turned my wailing into dancing; you removed my sackcloth and clothed me with joy..." (Psalm 30:11). He continues, "that my heart may sing to you and not be silent."

With the rapidly spreading publicity, Jesus has to take the man's isolation on himself. He can no longer enter the towns and villages where people are. He goes back to the loneliness of the wilderness. Yet in the wilderness Jesus attracts a wasteland of need. Takes on himself the suffering, not simply of one man, but of the world. To me the man, so long isolated by his illness, represents the whole world of the disadvantaged – the sick and dispossessed, the rootless and alienated, and as Christ shares the suffering of one person, he shares the suffering of all. People come to him from everywhere. Leaving their villages they seek him with new hope in their hearts. They bring their own brokenness to him and echo the words already spoken, "If you are willing..."

Perhaps we should remove the *if*. There's no uncertainty about it. He is willing. Whatever the condition, he stretches out his hand to touch the whole world. That *was* and *is* the reason he came to earth – to heal the wounds that hinder a deeper experience of God and help us recognise his Spirit at work in our lives, restoring the image in which we are made. We should never undervalue our life, or any life. It's God's gift and it gives us a dignity nothing and no-one else can. We can stand upright, not just physically but in the way we see ourselves. Whatever our circumstances each one of us is special – not in the sense of a supermarket special offer which tends to mean they are trying to sell something that isn't moving very fast – but in God's eyes. And even though everyone is special, its universality doesn't lessen its individuality.

The gift of life is God's, but we are invited to respond to it. We're not here simply to stand at the edge of the crowd and watch. We're part of that world, and as much part of the pain as we are of the healing process. In our response we create our own judgement. Not that we judge anyone.

It is, as Rowan Williams * has said, that we are judged by our victims and our response to them. When we raise barriers between ourselves and others, we become the persecutors. And the way we react to the people we find hard to accept, brings judgement on ourselves. We share a collective and individual responsibility for others because we share a common humanity. John Donne, the 16th century poet and cleric, wrote:

No man is an island, entire of itself;
every man is a piece of the Continent, a part of the main;
if a clod be washed away by the sea
Europe is the less
as well as if a promontory were...
any man's death diminishes me,
because I am involved in Mankind. **

We are diminished by the neglected suffering of others because we have shared in its creation. We share, too, a responsibility to do what we can to put things right. "We are God's workmanship," says St. Paul, "created in Christ Jesus to do good works." (Ephesians 2:10) And we're diminished by our inadequate and half-hearted responses. The spiritual challenge becomes a political and social challenge. And why not? If our spirituality doesn't take us into the world to struggle for justice and righteousness, what is its purpose?

* Resurrection *by Rowan Williams, published by Darton, Longman and Todd*
** Meditation XVII

Lord,
I cannot feel the pain
that you have felt,
still feel.
The pain you gather to yourself
and stand,
world-wounded
at the crisis point
where good and evil meet,
and face the struggle that it brings.

I cannot feel the misery
you felt,
still feel,
your shoulders aching
with the weight of suffering
you take upon yourself.

I cannot feel the agony of mind
you undergo,
the heartache scars
that love has carved
into your life.

I only know the scars are beautiful
to those with eyes to see,
and from them comes
the healing that I crave.
And though I've caused the pain,
share its responsibility,
your touch is still for me,
your healing just a breath away.
It's unbelievable,
but true.

And in the touch
I find again the will to sing,
the joy that comes
from knowing
you are on my side.
I thank you, Lord.

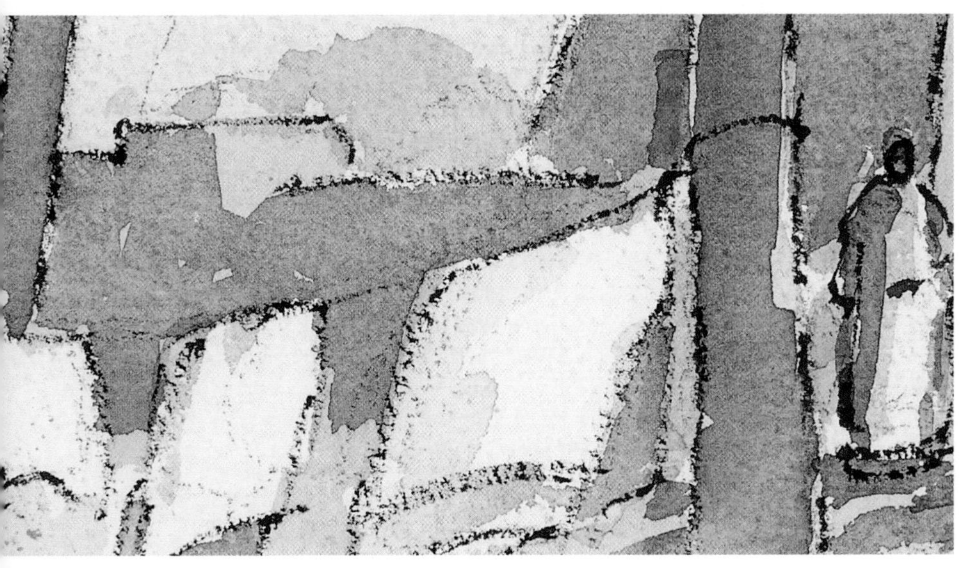

High Summer

Part Four

"Do not hold on to me."

Watercolour

Reading - John 19:41-John 20:18

At the place where Jesus was crucified, there was a garden, and in the garden a new tomb, in which no-one had ever been laid. Because it was the Jewish day of Preparation and since the tomb was near by, they laid Jesus there.

Early on the first day of the week, while it was still dark, Mary Magdalene went to the tomb and saw that the stone had been removed from the entrance. So she came running to Simon Peter and the other disciple, the one Jesus loved, and said, "They have taken the Lord out of the tomb, and we don't know where they have put him!"

So Peter and the other disciple started for the tomb. Both were running, but the other disciple outran Peter and reached the tomb first. He bent over and looked in at the strips of linen lying there but did not go in. Then Simon Peter, who was behind him, arrived and went into the tomb. He saw the strips of linen lying there, as well as the burial cloth that had been around Jesus' head. The cloth was folded up by itself, separate from the linen. Finally the other disciple, who had reached the tomb first, also went inside. He saw and believed. (They still did not understand from Scripture that Jesus had to rise from the dead.)

Then the disciples went back to their homes, but Mary stood outside the tomb crying. As she wept, she bent over to look into the tomb and saw two angels in white, seated where Jesus' body had been, one at the head and the other at the foot.
They asked her, "Woman, why are you crying?"
"They have taken my Lord away," she said, "and I don't know where they have put him." At this, she turned round and saw Jesus standing there, but she did not realise that it was Jesus.
"Woman," he said, "why are you crying? Who is it you are looking for?"
Thinking he was the gardener, she said, "Sir, if you have carried him away, tell me where you have put him, and I will get him."
Jesus said to her, "Mary." She turned towards him and cried out in Aramaic, "Rabboni!" (which means Teacher).
Jesus said, "Do not hold on to me, for I have not yet returned to the Father. Go instead to my brothers and tell them, 'I am returning to my Father and your Father, to my God and your God.'"
Mary Magdalene went to the disciples with the news: "I have seen the Lord!" And she told them that he had said these things to her.

Imagine...

It's early on Sunday morning and still dark. Mary wakes with a sigh to the sound of a cockerel crowing. The sigh comes from deep within her. She sits up, shivers, and rubs her arms in the cool room. It's been a restless night. She'd been lying there, drifting in and out of consciousness, exhausted, her mind refusing to shut down and rest. Vivid pictures of Jesus on the cross flash across her vision. Now she closes her eyes, wishing for a moment that she could blot it all out, get back under the blanket and forget, but she can't. "If only..." Her mind is a jumble of dark images, thoughts that get nowhere, but she takes another deep breath and gets up.

There are things to do. She looks out of the half-shuttered window. There's the first hint of dawn, red on the horizon, and closer to home a few dim lights flicker in neighbouring houses. She hears a voice, and another answering, in the street below, then the shuffle of animals in the courtyard. She smells the sharp smoke of early morning kitchen fires hovering, hardly moving in the still air, above the flat roofs of the houses. She splashes cold water on her face, combs her hair without thought or care – the routine actions which begin every day – and she's ready. Wrapping a shawl around her shoulders and picking up the spices she'd prepared the day before, she slips on her sandals and leaves the house.

She doesn't notice people sleeping curled in the doorways. She walks unseeing, her mind still heavy with grief. Saturday hadn't helped. It merely continued the nightmare of Friday and delayed the opportunity to weep over Jesus' body, to show her respect and love.

The main gates in the city walls are still closed but she slips through the tiny needle-gate, unbarred by a sleepy watchman. She finds the path to the tomb – she knows where it is, she'd been there on Friday – and the tomb was new, the marks of the mason's chisel still sharp and clear on the stone. By now there's a soft early morning light in the garden, and as she gets near she pauses, her hands tighten on the bundles she's carrying, and her eyes widen. The tomb is open. The stone's been moved. She stops, looks around, then goes nearer. The tomb is empty.

Early on the first day of the week, while it was still dark, Mary Magdalene went to the tomb and saw that the stone had been removed from the entrance.

John 20:1

It was just another ordinary day. People were stirring along the road as she passed. A few shopkeepers were opening up to catch the early trade. Nothing new in that. The garden was quiet. There was no-one there. Birds called in the trees as they always called. Sunlight was warming the ground as it always did, chasing the last of the mist away. Everything as usual. But not for Mary.

Mary began the day early – while it was still dark. She couldn't wait. Since she'd first met him, Jesus had filled her life. He'd accepted her without conditions, loved her as she was. Made her whole, helped her to love herself, to find new dignity and purpose in her life. She'd responded with a passionate love which nothing could alter. The men around Jesus had blown hot and cold. Sometimes they'd responded to his teaching with enthusiasm, at other times with questions and doubt. They'd misunderstood and quarrelled about their places in the coming kingdom. And in the confused confrontation in the darkness of Gethsemane they'd run away. Yes, run away. That was something she still couldn't accept. They'd left Jesus alone. Abandoned him. Not Mary. She'd stayed by the cross to the end. By his side. She was "glued to him" as Jean Vanier, founder of L'Arche communities, once said.

She'd watched Jesus die, felt the agony, seen every laboured breath and movement of muscle, and finally followed his body to the tomb. She was still numb, although a slow, weary acceptance of her loss was beginning to seep into her mind. This morning, with great courage and determination, she'd gathered the spices and cloths and set out for the garden.

There were practical questions to face. Who would move the stone? In passing I wonder why none of the men had gone with her to provide the muscle. Were they still in running-away mode? Still hiding and too frightened, or too ashamed? Maybe Mary was unwilling to wait for them. I wonder what had gone on between them all during the Sabbath. How did the men who'd run away face the women who had stayed with John at the cross? There must have been hurt feelings, recriminations, words spoken and other words left unsaid.

As Mary arrives at the tomb it's all very sad and low key, like a film in slow motion. Everyone – other gospel accounts tell us other women went with her – seems to move slowly, voices hushed. Then suddenly it's as though someone's pressed the fast-forward button and the film speeds up. Details vary – eye-witness accounts often do – but as they got nearer they saw the guards had disappeared, the stone had been rolled away, the tomb was empty.

It was the first day of the week. I take hold of the symbolism here. Jesus was laid in the tomb just before sunset, in the gathering dark, the end of the day. But now the morning light was chasing the darkness away. A new day was beginning. A new era. New. An adjective used to describe many things – a new tomb, a new commandment, a new covenant, a new creation, a new heaven and a new earth – but all that was still in the future, waiting to be understood. Mary had no inkling of it, no hint of reassurance yet. She was walking towards the point of transformation, where two worlds, divine and human, met and focused, and where our understanding of life and death would be changed forever. It was one of those "thin places" where "only a bit of tissue paper separates things spiritual from things material." * She was walking in sadness and despair towards a soon-to-be-revealed joy and hope.

But not quite yet. She was bewildered and could only interpret the scene in human terms. The stone was rolled away, the tomb was open and empty. Someone must have removed his body.

* *George MacLeod of Iona quoted by John Rackley in* Thin Places, *Open House Publications*

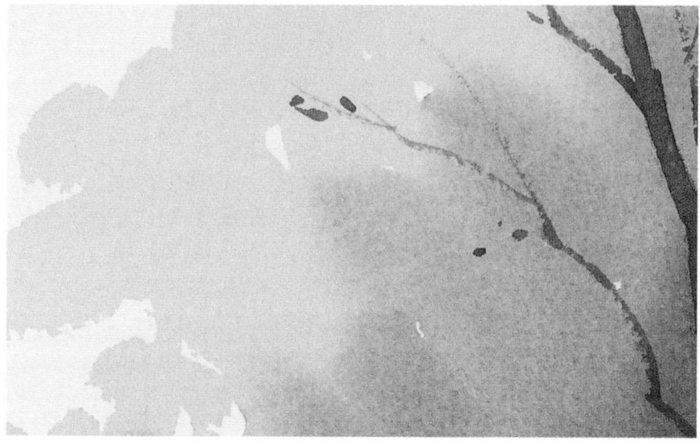

Lord, it's hard to wait.
To stand and gather up
the disconnected pieces of my life
and look for meaning,
try to fit them into place,
resolve the puzzle,
see it whole.

It's hard to wait.
To listen in the empty spaces of my life
for words and reassurances
that do not always come.
To wait for just one word
that says without a doubt
that you are here with me.
And as I stand within the garden
and before the empty tomb
of hopes and longings unfulfilled,
and though I cannot feel your presence close,
you stand with me,
one footstep out of vision,
willing me to lift my eyes and see.

It's hard for you to wait.
I wonder, are there moments
when you're tempted to give up on me?
To move away and find someone
a little less obtuse,
more malleable material to mould
and shape into the personality he's meant to be.

But, Lord, I know one thing,
and hold it tight through all the storms,
that you will never let me go.
That through the winds of questioning
that blow the leaves of doubt
to drift and build
within the corners of my life,
you still stand near, a breath away,
and I await and listen
for the moment
when you call my name.

Sunlight after Storm, Arneside *Pastel*

"Woman," he said, "why are you crying?
Who is it you are looking for?"

John 20:15

I wonder how Peter spent Saturday. Had he been crying too? I see him sitting hunched in a corner, hardly speaking, certainly not eating; staring blankly at the wall. Occasionally standing up and pacing the room, submerged in guilt. He'd found enough courage to follow the soldiers in the darkness but lost it when he was recognised in the firelight in the high priest's courtyard. (John 18:25-27) Now his mind was playing and replaying the memory of his denial, his lies, his failure.

Then early on Sunday morning, Mary runs back from the garden to Peter. She rushes up the stairs and bangs on the door. She went to him first. In spite of his denials, he was still the acknowledged leader of the disciples. She's breathless from running and from the shock of finding the tomb open and empty. Mary and Peter face each other in a meeting of opposites: the constant and the inconstant, the reliable and the unreliable, the joyful and the despairing. Yet Jesus had offered friendship to both. Welcomed, loved and accepted them for who they were, and for what they could each become.

Gasping for breath, Mary may not have been at her most coherent, but Peter, and then John, heard what she had to say. They looked at each other, questions in their eyes. What had really happened? Could it be true, or was Mary mistaken? They had to find out. Without any further word they made for the door, Mary following. The urgency made them run too. They were faster than Mary – she'd already run the road once – and by the time she reached the garden again, they'd already seen the empty tomb and gone to tell the others. Didn't they meet and pass Mary on the way back? Was there no more conversation? Perhaps just a shouted phrase as they passed her, the men not pausing in their haste.

She was left at the tomb, weeping. The tomb was open and empty so why did she stay? She'd gone early in the morning to care for Jesus but there was no body; so there was nothing for her to do. Wasn't it enough that they'd killed Jesus? Couldn't they at least have left his body in peace? Left it for her. Perhaps she felt as empty as the tomb. Jesus had been her life, now she was bereft, rootless. Nothing could have prepared her for this. I suggest she stayed because that's where he'd been. That's where she'd last seen him. Her whole being demanded that she stay near and at least try to find out where his body had been taken.

Then she sensed movement, just out of sight. She turned, her head bowed, wiping away the tears. She saw a man's feet, a gardener's feet. "Why are you crying?" he asked, echoing the question of the angels. She, who'd loved him so much, failed to recognise the voice. The last time she'd wept, she'd washed his feet with her tears and dried them with her hair. "He's gone," she sobbed, "they've taken him away." I doubt if she could have identified who *they* were, but we always need someone to blame, somebody to hold responsible for events outside our control. She was weeping for him, weeping for herself, weeping for all the love and hope she'd lost. Jesus had died; that was the end. Her grief didn't allow for the impossible. And at this moment all the pent-up emotion, building within her over the Sabbath, finds its release. The dam breaks and the tears pour out.

"Why are you crying?" he asked. Mary was the first person to meet the risen Jesus and to hear his voice. Why her? Because she was there, waiting. Creating, even without conscious purpose, the conditions in which he could speak to her. Yearning still for him, for his presence and his voice, as saints have yearned, as we yearn, for the Lord's presence. And as many saints have confirmed, even if we don't recognise his presence, the fact of our yearning is a sure sign of his presence already.

But immediately after the question "Why are you crying?" comes another question. "Who are you looking for?" And in this one gut-wrenching moment of bleak distress Jesus revealed himself to her. He came to her, as he comes to each one of us, in moments of our deepest weakness; hovering on the edge of our vision, offering his presence. Often coming in ways we find hard to recognise or acknowledge. He comes to us as a stranger, as he did to the two disciples on the Emmaus road (Luke 24: 13-35), and as he stood on the shore of Galilee (John 21:4). We are never left alone.

"Why are you crying?" A simple question but a profound one – many simple questions are. Why should she cry? Why should we cry? Jesus isn't dead, he's alive. The time for tears has gone. He's alive and his love has been released to cover the world. Christians are resurrection people, not Good Friday people. John Donne understood that. He wrote: "Our last day is our first day; our sunset is our morning; the day of our death is the first day of our eternal life." * If only we lived like that.

* *From* 50 Sermons, *published in 1649*

Lord, when I look around
beyond the ragged edges of my life
it's easy to despair.
To feel a void, an emptiness
that tempts me into thinking you're not there.
That life is empty and the meaning's gone.
That you have left the world
to manage on its own.
Left me to manage on my own.
Your presence nothing more
than folded grave clothes.
A fleeting memory and nothing more.
I wouldn't blame you
if you had left everything
and gone back home.
In fact, I think if I'd been in your place
that's just what I'd have done,
gone home
and left us to our own devices.
Except this is your home
as much as anywhere.
It only goes to show
that's why I'm where I am
and you are where you are.

I know you're here,
beside me even now
however much you seem to hide,
however quietly you speak,
or not at all.
You're there. You're here.
You seem to play a game of hide and seek
to draw me out and on,
to help me find you in new ways.
The air around is full of sounds
I can't quite catch.
And then a trick of light
that holds a presence just beyond my sight.
The moment may last longer
than my childhood's counting one to ten.

But when I search the bushes of my doubts,
peer through the trees,
look round the corner of my hesitations,
I find you standing there.
Not always in familiar ways I've known before,
sometimes more challenging
than comfortable,
but there.

And when I come to think of it,
if I could always feel you near
I'd miss the joy
of finding you again.

Jesus said to her, "Mary."

John 20:16

I try to imagine the deep surge of feeling that exploded in Mary's heart as she recognised the voice; the grief and anger gone in an instant. In a wave of excitement and love and hope she accepted the impossible immediately. She had no questions, no reservations, no doubts. Her heart recognised what her eyes had not. It was Jesus. He was there.

The other gospels tell us that the messengers at the tomb had said, "He is not here; he has risen!" (Matthew 28:6) But he *was* there, no longer lying inert in the tomb, but outside in the early morning quiet of the garden. Alive, vibrant. Mary cries out, but it's the one word that Jesus speaks that captures the imagination – her name. Mary, Mariam. Jesus called her by name. It was more personal than the word *woman* he'd used earlier. She'd heard him call her name many times. Asking for her help, thanking her, using it in conversation with other followers on the road.

Using her name holds a greater significance than we realise. God loves the whole of his creation with passion. A cosmic love. "The love that moves the sun and all the stars," as Dante wrote in *The Divine Comedy*. He loves its galaxies, the earth and sky, rain forests and plains, seas and rivers. And God loves the life he created, plants and animals, humankind. Then, God in Jesus loves his followers as a community; and he also loves each one of us as individuals. Loves Mary as Mary. Jesus called her by name. I hear echoes of the prophet Isaiah: "Fear not, for I have redeemed you; I have summoned you by name; you are mine." (Isaiah 43:1) The prophet recognises and rejoices in an intimacy between God and every part of his creation, between him and each one of us, a relationship even death cannot interrupt.

Sometimes God does seem far away. To Mary at the tomb, to me at my desk. Questions, hesitations, drop into the mind unasked, unwanted. One morning, I'd read something I only half understood and found hard to accept; my faith wouldn't stretch to cover it. I was sceptical, not unusual for me. "Am I on the right road?" I wondered. Earlier, I'd read those words in Isaiah almost mechanically, not really taking them in. A few minutes later, moving on in my reading, the words came again in a different context and suddenly I realised they related not just to Mary but to me. They were personal. "You are mine." A reassurance that turned my day round. God knows me by name. My personality is recognised and secure. I'm not simply a tiny part of an amorphous mass of humanity, I'm me.

God loves with unconditional love. It doesn't depend on our response. Even when we reject him he goes on loving us with a constancy, a stubbornness – there's no-one more stubborn than God – that allows nothing to get in the way. God loves because he *is* love. He can do no other. He may be all-powerful but he has set himself to work within the parameters of his love. God cannot *not* love. Love is the core of his nature and we are called to live out that nature. We are called not to judge and condemn, as Christians often seem prone to do, but to love and affirm. God sets no conditions on his love for us – except the one that says we can set no conditions either. As he accepts us as we are, so we can only accept him as he is. If we set conditions, we create God in our own image. And that's not God.

Mary recognises Jesus in the early morning light. She reaches out to him, arms wide. It's a natural reaction. Stand near the barrier at the railway station, or in the Arrivals hall at the airport and watch how people meet those they love. They touch, hug, kiss, hold. Mary hoped, expected, that he'd stretch his hand out as he'd done in the past. She'd seen him do it to so many – to the paralysed man, the blind, the man with leprosy. And her hands went out to him.

Lord,
As I grow older
I find it isn't easy any more
remembering another person's name.
I try.
I smile, shake hands
and try so hard
to register the name
and fit it to the face.
But give me half an hour
– that's wishful thinking, Lord,
I only need two minutes –
and I forget with startling efficiency.
I'm told by scientists it's not my fault,
something to do with nerve cells in my brain
and synapses that don't connect
the way they used to do.
It can be quite embarrassing
and sometimes
when I'm told we've met before
I can dredge up
no more than some vague recollection.

I thank you, Lord,
that's not the way you look at me.
You know my name.
I have your promise
that I'm recognised and treasured.
That you know me for who I am.
Not that I've any valid claim to recognition
but simply that your love embraces me
without reserve.
It's comforting as well
to realise your memory's reliable
and that you won't forget.

And Lord,
I have just one last thing to say:
whoever's name I can forget
with such facility,
it's never yours.
And that's a comfort.

Dead Sea, Israel

Watercolour

Jesus said, "Do not hold on to me..."

John 20:17

Mary reaches out to Jesus. "Don't hold on to me," he says. I try to hear the tone of voice. Was it a quick sharp word, an immediate reaction? Or a gentle, understanding murmur? Did he take a half-step back to put space between them or simply raise a hand? Whatever it was, it must have hurt Mary. However gently Jesus spoke, it would have felt like a rejection, clouding, just for a moment, her surge of joy. Learning experiences may be happy or painful. God is in both, willing our good. She'd been so close to Jesus. He'd transformed her life. Then on Friday she'd stood and watched his agony on the cross. Now her emotions were in freefall, turned upside down in the heart-stopping joy of seeing him alive again. What more natural than for her to want to take up the relationship again, just as it had been? But that couldn't be. Relationships are never static. They grow and change as we do, absorbing and being shaped by our experiences along the way.

Mary had to learn, as we all have to learn, that she can't simply hold on to the Jesus she first knew. He was asking her to grow up; to develop a new and deeper relationship with him. She'd been so dependent. Following him as one of the group, her decisions made for her, going where and when he determined to go. Now she had to face a painful time of change as she moved towards maturity. To learn to trust and experience a Jesus she would be unable to see but who would still be close. Perhaps too, there's a sense in which Mary was trying unconsciously to control Jesus. To pigeonhole him, keep him classified and manageable. It's more comfortable that way; to have a predictable God who does everything the way we want him to. But it's a sure way to lose him.

In one of her songs, that great American singer, Barbra Streisand, sings to her lover, "If you ever leave me, will you take me with you?" Literally impossible of course, but it captures a longing never to be parted from one you love. And deeper, it suggests a paradox of Christian experience. God's apparent absence only hides his presence. Through it he seeks to draw us into a closer, deeper relationship. When God leaves us, he does indeed take us with him.

Growing into maturity is a process that never ends. Jesus was asking Mary to loosen the tight grip she held on what she knew, and reach out into the unknown. He asks us too, to think for ourselves, to make our own decisions. Commitment to Jesus doesn't shift the responsibility for our lives onto him. The poet, T.S.Eliot, understood this. He wrote: "For us, there is only the trying. The rest is not our business." * We follow the Way, make our own decisions and do our best. The rest is in God's hands.

Mary would find it a closer and more challenging relationship than anything that had gone before; and that goes for all of us. Faith is about change and growth. It needs space and time to mature. A plant changes shape as it grows – you only have to look at our overcrowded shrubbery to see the truth of that. God wants us to grow. And the only way to grow is to recognise that what we know and experience isn't final, that our understanding is partial. "Now we see but a poor reflection as in a mirror; then we shall see face to face. Now I know in part; then I shall know fully, even as I am fully known." (1 Corinthians 13:12) In Biblical times mirrors weren't made of glass but of polished metal – copper or silver – and the reflections were dim.

Loosening our grip on what we know doesn't deny earlier experience but opens us to the possibility of a deeper understanding of God's truth. He wants us to move on. It's reassuring to stay in the comfort of familiar spiritual landscapes but it doesn't get us far. God is an uncomfortable God; always inviting us to adventure, to break new ground in our faith. I confess I have a problem with fundamentalist thought that chains itself to the past; in wishing to preserve everything exactly as it was. In the end, rather than our protecting the past, the past may begin to enslave us.

There's always more to learn. The Welsh poet, R.S. Thomas wrote:

He is such a fast God,
Always before us and
Leaving as we arrive... **

God is continually dancing along my path, beckoning me on, encouraging me to explore greater depths of his love. Faithfulness is about following, travelling, searching, not standing still.

* *T.S.Eliot* Four Quartets, *East Coker*
** *R.S.Thomas* Pilgrimages, *Collected Poems 1945-1990, published by Phoenix*

Lord, you make me feel uncomfortable.
You rarely seem to work
the way I think you should.
You constantly surprise me
doing things in ways
I never thought to see.
You stand there
in the shadow of my thoughts
and when, not knowing where to go,
I turn, put out my hand,
I find you're out of reach.
Not far.
Still near enough to love
but just a bit too far to touch.
And in the hair's-breadth distance
there is room for me to grow
in my relationship with you.

If I could have my way –
I'm fantasising now –
I'd like you more predictable.
A routine God whose switches I could press
and find a strong and comforting espresso
poured in my life
just as and when I need it.

But no, not you.
You ask me to grow up,
to put away the childish things,
make my own way,
my own decisions.
It sometimes feels
as though I'm on my own,
but that's not true, I know.
You're offering me the chance,
the God-sent opportunity –
the your-sent opportunity –
to grow into maturity.
To be the grown-up personality
I'm meant to be.
It may not mean a comfortable life
but this I know – it is exciting.

"Go instead to my brothers and tell them, 'I am returning to my Father and your Father, to my God and your God.'" Mary Magdalene went to the disciples with the news: "I have seen the Lord!" And she told them that he had said these things to her.
John 20:17-18

Mary was the first person to see the risen Jesus. She was the first to hear his voice; the first to speak to him, and to be given a message to pass on to his friends. And Mary was a woman. I'd love to know whose feathers that ruffled among the male disciples. Jesus had always been surprising, and he was continuing that way. He could never be confined within a set of rules, although many of his followers over the next 20 centuries have tried hard to do so. Yet however we try to control him, however tight the prison, he will burst through the doors of our conventions and bring freedom – not only for himself but for his followers.

He gave Mary a message of good news to pass on – she was the first post-resurrection evangelist – and what good news it was. Through Jesus' death and resurrection the door to God's kingdom is wide open. "Go to my brothers" he said – and I'm sure he included sisters too. The family bond is confirmed. The relationship which Jesus enjoyed with God, and which he expressed in calling him *Abba*, father, is offered to all of them, and to each one of us. "I am going to *my* Father and *your* Father, to *my* God and *your* God." The intimacy with God, which Jesus enjoyed, is offered to all. An astonishing possibility which takes the breath away. The stone which stood between God and his creation is rolled away, Eden's locked gate is open once more.

The love in which Jesus lived can be ours and can give us the power to live for him; to change and to grow. That grace doesn't come ready-made. It calls for effort, and evangelists who claim it's easy do the kingdom of God little service. There's still struggle. It's no quick fix. The growth process lasts a lifetime and is never completed, but there is joy and fulfilment in the journey.

Living and preaching in the 17th century, the English poet John Donne, whom I've quoted before, wrote:

Here in this world
so far as I can enter into my master's sight
I can enter into my master's joy.

continued overleaf

I can see God
in his creatures,
in his church,
in his word and sacraments and ordinances;
since I am not without this sight,
I am not without this joy.
I cannot put off mortality,
but I can look upon immortality;
I cannot depart from this earth,
but I can look into heaven.

In this developing relationship, we begin to see the world through new eyes, to identify the presence of God all around us. Sometimes it's shadowy, on the edge of vision, at other times crystal-clear. There's joy when we catch a glimpse of it, when we hear the echo of it, even though we must wait for the fullness still to come. And as we grow closer to him, we realise that this relationship isn't a transplant from outside. The presence of God is already within us, waiting to be released, waiting to flood and transform the depths of our being.

The poet Wordsworth felt it when he wrote: "But trailing clouds of glory do we come from God, who is our home." * Much of life is routine, but at times moments of transcendence may break through, and a feeling of the presence of God can suddenly overwhelm. I was walking the dog late one cold winter night. The sky was clear, the stars brilliant. There would be a frost. I stood still to take it all in. Suddenly the whole earth seemed to expand and I felt a great sense of wonder. My smallness seemed caught up into the immensity of God and his universe. I had no words, they weren't needed. The whole experience lasted only a few seconds (or was it a lifetime?) but I've carried the wonder with me ever since.

And I believe Mary carried the wonder of God's presence with her through the rest of her life. She finds new life at the entrance to the empty tomb – or should we now call it the exit from the tomb?

* *Wordsworth,* Intimations of Immortality

I stand like Mary, Lord,
before the empty tomb
and questions come unbidden.
I do not, cannot, know
the how and why.
This is your doing
and I can only stand in awe
and wait.
And hope that when you call my name
as you called hers,
I'll recognise the voice
and know I'm known by you.
Come and reveal yourself
– as gardener if you will.
Dig, plant and prune my life
until it fruits
in recognition of your presence,
the door-stone of my fears rolled back,
my life renewed.

I wish that I could see you as she did
but though I cannot see you with my eyes
I hear the whispers of your presence everywhere.
Earth is alive with echoes of your love,
your rainbowed beauty's treasures far and near.
Hints of your glory spread
in children's innocence,
in lovers' joy,
in lives lived well,
in those who fight
for justice and for truth.

And in the distance, Lord,
I think I see
the garden gates of Eden
open once again.
And you are there to welcome.
Alleluia.

Quiet Water

Part Five

The courage to be honest

Watercolour

Reading - John 11:16

Then Thomas (called Didymus) said to the rest of the disciples, "Let us also go, that we may die with him."

Reading - John 14:1-6

"Do not let your hearts be troubled. Trust in God; trust also in me. In my Father's house are many rooms; if it were not so, I would have told you. I am going there to prepare a place for you. And if I go and prepare a place for you, I will come back and take you to be with me that you also may be where I am. You know the way to the place where I am going."

Thomas said to him, "Lord, we don't know where you are going, so how can we know the way?"

Jesus answered, "I am the way and the truth and the life. No-one comes to the Father except through me."

Reading - John 20:24-29

Now Thomas (called Didymus), one of the Twelve, was not with the disciples when Jesus came. So the other disciples told him, "We have seen the Lord!"

But he said to them, "Unless I see the nail marks in his hands and put my finger where the nails were, and put my hand into his side, I will not believe it."

A week later his disciples were in the house again, and Thomas was with them. Though the doors were locked, Jesus came and stood among them and said, "Peace be with you!" Then he said to Thomas, "Put your finger here; see my hands. Reach out your hand and put it into my side. Stop doubting and believe."

Thomas said to him, "My Lord and my God!"

Then Jesus told him, "Because you have seen me, you have believed; blessed are those who have not seen and yet have believed."

Imagine...

Sunday evening. It's dark and the disciples are together again in the upstairs room. There's a bright moon in the sky but they've closed all the shutters so that the light from the small oil lamps can't be seen outside. They're all there, except for Thomas – and Judas. Thomas hasn't come and no-one seems to know where he is. They aren't at ease in the room; it holds too many recent memories. They can still see Jesus in their imaginations, and their last meal together. The way he'd taken water and a towel and washed their feet. It had made them uncomfortable then, but now it was worse. Their desertion a few hours later when Jesus had been arrested didn't bear thinking about. And the words he'd spoken during supper kept coming back like indigestion, but still they can't understand them.

They're confused and frightened. They are, most of them, country folk. Intelligent but unsophisticated. They're without influence, ordinary men and women out of their depths in both the secular and religious politics of Jerusalem. The air is full of regrets and guilt. Questions too. That morning, Peter and John had seen the empty tomb. There'd been talk of angels, and Mary Magdalene was convinced that Jesus was alive and free. She'd seen him, so she said, and she'd brought a message from him but still... It was too much to take in. They wanted it to be true but could they really believe what she was saying?

They'd locked the door. They're still afraid and every time they hear a noise out in the street they stiffen, tense and waiting. Suddenly and silently Jesus is there. There is no knock, nothing to startle them, just his presence. One moment he wasn't there, the next he is. He seems to expand and fill the room. They stand or sit where they are, eyes wide, mouths open, no movement and no words – until Jesus moves and speaks. Then they see his wounds and hear the voice saying again what he had so often said, "Peace be with you."

Peace. Was that possible for them? Wonder and joy bubble up to the surface of their minds and they reach out to touch and hold and take him back into their lives. Then there's a pause, a drawing back, as Jesus looks at each one of them. The still-raw memories flood in – memories of what they'd done, or hadn't done, the night he was betrayed and they had run

continued overleaf

away. Behaviour that had to be faced and lived through. Suddenly, the silence is broken. Several of them speak at once.

"Lord, we're so ashamed..." Jesus interrupts. "Peace," he says.
"We were afraid..." "Peace," he says, more firmly.
"What can we do to prove...?" "Peace," he says again.

And there is quiet. Words are no longer needed. Jesus is with them. There are no recriminations. No anger or accusations. He looks at each one of them, a hint of a smile on his face. And in that moment the peace they feel is real; it goes deep down. A moment none of them will ever forget.

Then Thomas (called Didymus) said to the rest of the disciples, "Let us also go, that we may die with him."

John 11:16

We're unfair to Thomas. We call him Doubting Thomas. I prefer to call him Honest Thomas. You knew where you stood with him. He was transparent. If he disagreed he said so. If he didn't understand he asked questions. Not the brightest intellect, but he was open and loyal.

When Jesus decided to go back to Judea – read it for yourself in John 11 – the disciples didn't like the idea. It all began with news of the death of a friend, Lazarus. His home was in Bethany, near Jerusalem. The city and the area around were dangerous for Jesus, and later events would prove just how dangerous they were. In earlier visits he'd challenged the power of the religious establishment. He'd stirred up serious opposition and only just escaped with his life. In human terms returning to Jerusalem was foolish, reckless, and the disciples tried to argue Jesus out of going. The Gospel narrative cleans it up a bit into a gentle question-and-answer session. I believe it was more than that – it was a more full-blooded disagreement. In imagination I see the disciples tense and concerned, Jesus quiet but determined. It was a real difference of opinion. They're protective, trying to change his mind. "It's for your own good," they say. "If you go back there you'll be asking for trouble. They'll take you and kill you." And in the back of their minds I suspect they were thinking, "And us too."

How quick we can be deciding what's best for other people, and often it seems to coincide with our own needs. The way we pray can mirror the attitude of the disciples. It can be easier to pray for a change in circumstance rather than ask for the strength to make the most of where we are. Sister Wendy Beckett, Anglican nun and art critic, once wrote, "We pray not to have the course of nature changed but to be helped to see in that course what God intends for us and to use it to grow in love and joy." Prayer can help us accept what we don't like, and use what we can't understand, if we allow it to.

But back to the story. Jesus will not be diverted from the path he's chosen. He gets ready to go, and it's now that Thomas shows his loyalty and courage. I see him sigh, raise his eyebrows, shrug his shoulders – not necessarily in Jesus' direct line of sight – and say, "That's enough. You

continued overleaf

won't change him. We either stay here and let him go alone, or we go with him." And after a brief pause, he adds, "And I'm going with him." Thomas was ready to face the danger rather than abandon Jesus.

They could all have refused to go. Earlier, when Jesus' teaching had become too challenging, many followers had left him, and he had turned to the Twelve and asked if they too would leave. Then, it was Simon Peter who'd answered, "Lord, to whom shall we go. You have the words of eternal life." (John 6:66-68) Perhaps Thomas was hearing an echo of those words in his own heart and, although he didn't understand, he was unwilling to turn back. You couldn't call Thomas an optimist. He could only see a tragic end to the journey, but he was prepared to go with Jesus and face whatever might come. He was committed.

Lord,
life without you
would be impossible for me
but life with you does not come easy.
You make demands.
Your voice is velvet-soft
and one in theory I could choose to ignore
but your persistence makes resistance hard.
I know I'm free to choose
and there are times I use that freedom
in ways that are not yours,
but something, someone,
deep inside my heart
points me another way.

I hesitate.
I wish I could respond wholeheartedly.
The problem is
I'm very good at seeing all the snags,
the half-formed images of what might be.
The dangers lurking,
the shadows flickering
on the bedroom wall
that threatened childhood dreams,
now magnified.

The alternatives seduce
and tempt me into other paths
that offer safety, so it seems,
and less commitment.
But always, Lord,
my compass settles back
and points to you, true north,
the point to which I can direct my steps
in confidence if not in comfort.
And come what may
I'll stay with you.

What counts is faithfulness, not winning.
And when I come to think about it
to lose with you is really winning anyway.
Life isn't always easy
but there's a strength
I cannot find elsewhere.
I'll stick with it, Lord,
and with you.

Thomas said to him, "Lord, we don't know where you are going, so how can we know the way?" Jesus answered, "I am the way and the truth and the life."

John 14:5-6

It's not always comfortable standing out from the crowd. Easier to go along with the majority, keeping quiet when you disagree. It can be embarrassing too, to interrupt with a question that shows you've not understood what you've heard. Someone said it's better to keep quiet and be thought a fool than to open your mouth and prove it. Asking questions can mark you out but it's the way to learn. It's not always easy even within a Christian community, perhaps especially within a Christian community. Questions can be taken for a lack of faith, although faith built without some understanding may be weak and vulnerable anyway.

The disciples had gathered together in the upper room for what was to be their last meal before Jesus' death. Anticipating what lay ahead, Jesus was trying to strengthen and encourage them. It wasn't easy preparing them for the cataclysmic changes they would face at his departure. *En-courage*: to put courage into them. They would need it. Now they were puzzled and slow to understand. "You know the way," he said, calling on his reserves of patience. Apparently even Jesus found it difficult at times to move his followers out of their small expectations and broaden their vision. Little has changed!

Thomas had the courage to be honest. "Sorry, Lord," he said, maybe with a hint of exasperation in *his* voice, "I don't understand. It's beyond me." Actually he seems to have used the plural. "*We* don't understand." "We don't know where you're going," he protested, "so how can we know the way?" He could simply have been using the plural to shelter within the crowd, but I believe he was speaking for all of them, and they were content to let him act as mouthpiece and take the responsibility.

Jesus' answer was clear. Not "I'll show you where to go." He wasn't pointing them to a road they were to follow. "I am the way," he said. What a claim. He wouldn't give them a detailed route map; he was offering them a presence. They were to live as he lived, to take on his spirit, to live in his freedom. Though they wouldn't be able to see him he would still be with them on the journey. He would expect them to make their own decisions and to witness through their lives to the truth they'd received from him. In his novel *Merlin*, Stephen Lawhead writes: "This is our work in creation: to decide. And what we decide is woven into the thread of time and being forever. Choose wisely then, but you must choose." Their lifestyle would be distinctive and relevant wherever they were, whenever they lived. Early Christians were sometimes called 'Followers of the Way'; again not as a marked-out and predictable path but as a living-out of the presence of his spirit within them. They wouldn't be *following* Jesus into the truth, nor would he be taking them on *towards* new life at some future rendezvous. He was, is, the way, the truth, the life. They would be living it. The wonder of it, its breathtaking audacity, may have been hard for Thomas and his friends to take in but it was something they would grow into.

We're not told how Thomas and the others reacted to his words. I reckon we're only seeing the edge of a longer conversation with questions and answers; perhaps with more questions than answers. Some of the parameters of our life's path are set by circumstances we can't control, but we have freedom to choose the way we live within them. "I am the way," says Jesus. And when, like Thomas, we don't understand? Just go straight on doing what we are doing. The confirmation often comes later. The Danish philosopher, Sören Kierkegaard, wrote: "Life can only be understood backwards, but it must be lived forwards." There are many occasions when our minds are unsure and questioning, but our hearts know.

Christians don't have clear answers to every question – only the dangerous cults claim that – and it's foolish to pretend we have. Someone said, "Always seek the truth but carefully avoid anyone who claims to have all of it." Far better to admit to questions than to use a smokescreen of pious platitudes to mask our ignorance. People will see through the platitudes anyway, and so does God. If we are living out the Way, our lifestyle will be a far better witness to his presence than our words alone. Indeed, if our lifestyle doesn't authenticate our words then there's little point in talking. As St. Francis of Assisi is reputed to have told his followers, "Always preach the Gospel; if necessary use words." And I would add, "And ask questions."

Lord,
you are the way.
However much I add
my own interpretation to the words,
that's still the bottom line.
It might be easier
if you could give a chart,
clear and concise
to guide me in straight lines of certainty.
Then I could sail serenely
through the sand banks,
reefs and rocks of life
without a question or a doubt.
Unsinkable.

Or maybe not.
I might set out in misplaced confidence
and sail the straightest line
from one mistake to next.
Your gift is much more precious
than the certainty I think I'd like.
You offer freedom.
The opportunity each day
to choose my course,
to set my own direction,
to explore and know the joy
of new discovery.

At times it scares me, Lord,
that you have confidence in me
enough to set me free
and let me make my own decisions.
But though I'm free to make my choice
you don't abandon me.

Lord,
you are the way.
Not simply final destination
but journey too.
And as I travel on
I sense your presence.
Your life in mine, my life in yours,
dovetailed and intimate.
And when I cannot see the way ahead
with all the clarity I'd like,
give me the grace to trust.
That is the hardest part at times,
but, Lord, if you trust me
then surely I am right
to put my trust in you.

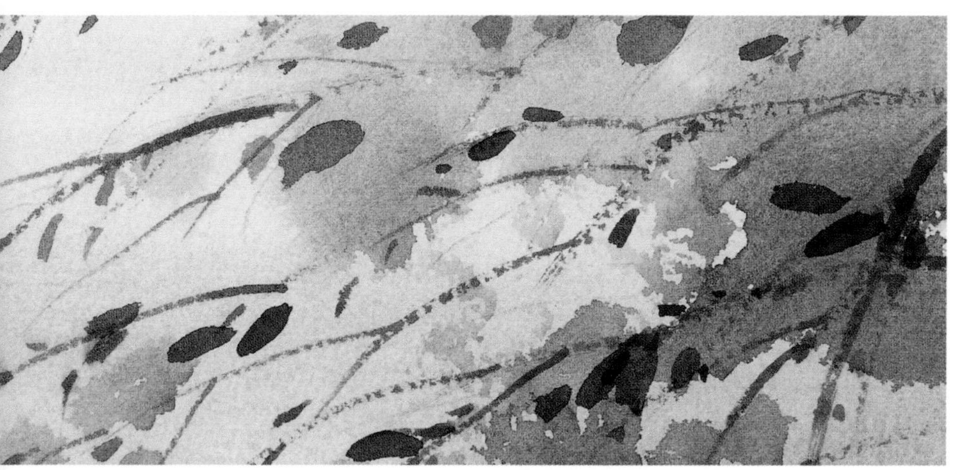

Weeping Willow

Watercolour

Now Thomas (called Didymus), one of the Twelve,
was not with the disciples when Jesus came.
So the other disciples told him, "We have seen the Lord!"
John 20:24-25

We don't know where Thomas was that resurrection morning, or why he wasn't with the others in the upper room. It's another of those intriguing mysteries the Bible holds. Maybe, after Jesus had died, Thomas had said "I told you so" once too often to be popular with the others. He'd been the one who'd warned that it would be dangerous for Jesus to go to Jerusalem, and his worst fears had come true. Or was it that he found being with them all, too difficult to cope with? Did he simply want to get away from them, to find a quiet place to grieve alone; curl up with his misery and anger and disillusionment? For whatever reason, Thomas had gone off on his own and had missed out on the big event.

First, Mary had met Jesus in the garden. Then the two travellers on the Emmaus road had rushed back to Jerusalem to tell of their meeting with him and, while they were talking this through, Jesus had appeared to everyone in the room.

Later, when Thomas joined them, he found the atmosphere had changed dramatically. The mourning, the mood of despair, had been transformed. Thomas was suddenly surrounded by excited people bombarding him with the news. He was bewildered and defensive. It wasn't what he'd expected. He couldn't take it in and he certainly couldn't join in the excitement. Some things are possible, others not. "No, no," he says, "wait a minute. Let's get this straight." Their eagerness had the opposite effect to the one they'd hoped for. Does this tell us something about our evangelism today? The rush of words didn't convince him. He'd seen Jesus heal the sick, the blind, the lame. He'd survived storms at sea with Jesus, but this was a step too far; a leap of faith he couldn't make. I imagine the disciples' exasperation with him and his growing stubbornness. "Unless I see for myself..." he said, and asked for proof and reassurance in the most solid form he could think of.

Some people have no problem with faith and feel no need to question anything. They hold a simple trust in God that carries them through the whole of life. That doesn't prevent problems or pain – these come to all of us whether we have faith or not, it's part of being human – but nothing weakens their faith in God's goodness, or masks the experience of Jesus in their lives.

For others faith doesn't come easily. When the latest tragedy is headlined in the newspapers and shouted out on television – an air crash, war, famine – many of us ask, "Why, Lord? If you are a loving God what does this mean? Where were you?" And when there's no immediate reply we wonder if God is even listening. Is he still there? There are times when he doesn't seem to be around any more. When we no longer feel the closeness we once felt and we seem to be surrounded by empty space. That's when we hang on to our faith by our fingernails. But God has a purpose in it and it's the seeming absence which tests us and, in a strange way, can strengthen us. Anthony de Mello, the Singhalese Jesuit, suggests that every painful event contains in itself a seed of growth and liberation, and our questioning may be part of the process. Jesus himself experienced the depths of loneliness on the cross. "My God, my God, why have you forsaken me?" he cries in agony. (Mark 15:34) If Jesus had moments of great doubt, can we expect to avoid them?

When doubts come, it's better to face them than pretend they don't exist. There's little point in pretending anyway – God already knows – and I believe that honest questioning can bring us closer to the Kingdom than any pretence of faith. Thomas' honesty in admitting his doubt was the last stepping stone that brought him face to face with Jesus and helped him cross the river of doubt into true belief.

Lord,
There's no point in pretending.
Doubts creep uninvited,
crowd the room,
push out the faith
I hold so tenuously.
Unanswered questions
play through my mind,
the volume amplified
with every repetition.
Why is it, Lord,
that you so often seem content
to let my queries go unheard,
with no reply
when just one word
would be enough to quell my fears?
My faith, ephemeral as candle smoke,
drifts and disperses
on the first faint breeze of doubt.

The only thing that gives encouragement –
one fact I can't deny –
is this:
that even in the midst of doubt
I still come back to you
and wait to meet you
in the upper room of my own life.

At times
I am exhausted by the struggle,
my mind a blank,
and then I hear
your voice say quietly
in words so soft
I'm not quite sure
they're there at all,
"I know. I felt the same."
That's all I need to hear.
And in its reassurance
I realise that I am loved just as I am.
That honest doubt's no barrier to love,
and in your love
my doubts and fears are gathered up,
my questions and anxieties accepted,
and though at times
the clouds and mist
may still obscure the path
you walk with me,
and though my feet may falter
and my grip on you grow weak,
you'll never let me go.

But he (Thomas) said to them, "Unless I see the nail marks
in his hands and put my finger where the nails were,
and put my hand into his side, I will not believe it."
John 20:25

I'm sure Thomas wanted to believe. He'd followed and loved Jesus – maybe not with the intensity of Mary Magdalene's love, but loved anyway – from earlier days. He wanted to believe that all he'd lived and worked for with Jesus, all he'd risked, wasn't wasted, hadn't come to an end. But the disciples were asking a lot of him. After all, they'd seen Jesus for themselves, he hadn't. They were asking Thomas to take it on trust, to accept their word for it. That was harder. It was just too big a step for him to take. All his hopes had died when Jesus died. He couldn't risk a resurrection of those hopes only for them to be dashed again when the excitement cooled and reality stepped in.

The exasperation levels among the disciples must have been high. Nothing they could say would convince Thomas; and possibly the more they said, the more he resisted. There's a time to speak and a time to allow silence to do its work. (Ecclesiastes 3:7) A time to allow people to chill out and think things through without pressure; to begin the inner journey which shows us our need, and helps us identify and accept the solution.

Thomas could have pretended. He could have gone along with them in their excitement. It would have been easier for him to keep quiet, to say nothing, to accept all they were saying without question. But that wasn't his way. There was a disconcerting openness about him. He expressed his feelings and doubts with courage and honesty. It's an honesty which some find difficult to deal with in the church today. Newcomers are welcomed – usually – but then they're expected to conform, to accept our behaviour and standards as the norm and settle down as one of the crowd. Their individuality can be disconcerting, and it can be uncomfortable to be asked the reasons behind habits that have grown over the years into hard-set rules.

When someone older in the faith has questions, it can be even more difficult to talk about them. We're expected to be firm in belief, to have no doubts or hesitations, and if we express them we might be met with criticism and disapproval rather than understanding. But is church only for perfect people, or is there a welcome for those who struggle on the way? We have to live with our human frailty. We're not all made to the same pattern and I'm sure that the God who made us knows that his gift of faith is more easily accepted by some than by others. Thomas mirrors the experience of many, and when I put myself in his shoes – although he'd probably have slipped them off at the door as he entered the room – I think I would have reacted the way he did.

Doubt can take many forms. There are some who deliberately refuse to believe, who turn away from the truth because it asks for too much change. Others hold honest doubts and simply ask for some tangible reassurance before committing themselves. And some have a real desire to believe but find it difficult to make a leap of faith into the unknown – which is the only way to prove its truth.

Thomas was a twin. *Thomas* is Hebrew for twin, as his other name, *Didymus*, is in Greek. We know nothing of his brother (or was it a sister?) nor of the rest of his family, but it seems to me that Thomas himself is a pair of twins. "Doubt and faith are twin brothers," says Khalil Gibran, and Thomas struggles with both. Finding faith is an honest battle for many. Questions come unbidden and rather than blame them on temptation – Satan's a great fallback, the one we blame when, often, we should be taking the responsibility ourselves – I see questions as a genuine and ongoing search for the truth. They certainly were for Thomas. Sydney Carter, poet and songwriter, said that "doubt is what you drown in or walk upon, the solid deck is never really solid."

I am convinced that God understands. A great Christian mystic said that the desire to desire God is taken for the fact and we need never despair. Why some people find it easier to walk a life of faith than others remains a mystery. At times, God seems quite comfortable not answering our questions, and when we ask for proof or justification he simply points to Jesus and says nothing else. A great Archbishop of Canterbury, Michael Ramsey, once wrote, "I want to want to want to want you, God." An expression of a continuing and honourable fight to hold the faith.

Lord,
I too am twins.
My life's a circus
and I rush around the ring
riding two horses,
one foot on faith, precarious at best,
the other finding foothold difficult in doubt,
each movement of the act uncertain.
At times I fall.
I try to keep my balance
but still I need
a firmer reassurance
than you're prepared to offer.
Encouragement
to face another skirmish
in the fight of faith,
while I'm still bruised
from earlier falls.

The wonder of it is
that in some way I hardly comprehend,
each time I end up gasping on the ground,
a hand, your hand, still scarred,
is there to lift me, dust me down,
return me to the ride.
It isn't easy
but one thing I know,
I won't give up.
I'll fight for little victories,
one at a time,
until I'm safely home with you,
and then together
we'll have one last laugh
at all the fuss I made
about so little.

A week later his disciples were in the house again, and Thomas was with them. Though the doors were locked, Jesus came and stood among them and said, "Peace be with you!" Then he said to Thomas, "Put your finger here; see my hands. Reach out your hand and put it into my side. Stop doubting and believe."

John 20:26-27

There's a silence in the story. A week had gone by, a week about which we know nothing. Another of those empty spaces my imagination tries to fill. Where were they all – Mary and John and Peter? How did Thomas get through that week? How did he cope with his inner conflict, the certainty of his friends and his own questions? Were they all trying to make sense of those strange words Jesus had spoken to them about forgiveness; or trying to come to terms with the effects of the Holy Spirit in their lives?

What was Jesus doing during the week? For some reason he was giving the disciples a breathing space. He refused to crowd in on them. There was only so much change they could cope with at once, especially after the turmoil of the crucifixion and the drama of the resurrection. There'd been so much of his teaching they couldn't understand when he'd been alive with them, but this was mind-blowing. Life after death. They needed time to work through it. As the week went on and Sabbath came and went again, I sense a growing tension and expectancy. Jesus had risen on Sunday, the day after Sabbath, had appeared to them on that same day, and now it was Sunday again.

This time Thomas was with them. I try to imagine his reaction when Jesus appeared. I see him standing, still as a statue, his face pale with shock, his heart racing. "Shalom," says Jesus, "Peace." A standard greeting but one with a special meaning today, particularly for Thomas. "I'm bringing you peace, Thomas. I'm here to show you the truth, to set your doubts at rest." The wonder is that Jesus doesn't reproach or rebuke him. He doesn't accuse Thomas of disloyalty; he makes no attempt to shame him or make him feel guilty. I reckon there was no need to underline it. Thomas must have felt all of this as he stood before Jesus.

Jesus so often surprises us, but the one thing that we *can* predict is that whatever he does, he does with love. "Thomas," says Jesus, his voice gentle, " If you need to touch me, here are my hands." At that moment I wonder if Thomas' mind flashed back to that last supper he'd shared with Jesus? "This is my body given for you. This is my blood poured out for you," he'd said. Once again, the hands that touched the blind man and the leprosy victim are stretched out, this time to heal Thomas. In an instant Thomas' eyes are opened and he steps firmly into the community of believers.

There was a challenge too in what Jesus said and did. "I'm real," says Jesus, "and if you take hold of me now we can deal with your doubts together." And in showing his wounds to Thomas, Jesus is strengthening the faith of all the others gathered in the room. Thomas' doubts and questions become a positive blessing to them all.

We're not told whether Thomas actually touched Jesus. My own reading and imagination tells me that he didn't; that there was no need. Once he was confronted by the living Christ his doubts drained away and he was led to make the greatest statement of faith anyone could make. His battle was over.

Lord,
My hands should bear the wounds,
not yours.
The scars of guilt
for all the things I should have done
but haven't,
and all the things I shouldn't do
but have.
Yours are the hands of innocence,
the hands of loving kindness,
strong and true,
which offer restoration
to my careworn spirit.
Sometimes I think there's two of me,
that deep inside my being
there's the sound
of some wild cosmic battle being fought,
of good and ill.
A war of faith and doubt.
At times I am a warrior in the fight,
and in confusion
taking first one side and then the other.
At other times I'm just the battlefield
on which the struggle's set
and I am pushed around
by forces I cannot control
however hard I try.

But still I trust, Lord,
still cling with all my little strength
to you,
my one firm hope
that though the struggle's hard at times,
and final victory may lie far ahead,
you'll cling to me
and never let me go.

Yours are the hands of innocence,
the hands of loving kindness,
strong and true.

Watercolour

Thomas said to him, "My Lord and my God!"
John 20:28

This moment would be etched deep into the fabric of Thomas' being for the rest of his life. The moment when Jesus, his teacher, the man he'd lived with for three years, suddenly revealed himself to Thomas with a graciousness beyond words. Thomas responds in the only way possible, "My Lord and my God." The words seem to shout from the page in triumph, but I hear Thomas almost whispering them in awe, taking them into the deepest corners of his heart. His eyes are focused on Jesus, all his attention fixed on him. The questions, the scepticism, are swamped in a great flood of joy and love. It's a moment of release as his hesitations and inhibitions, the deadweight of all his doubts, fall away. And it's two-way. Not simply a moment when Thomas accepts Jesus for who he is, but the moment when Thomas realises that, complete with his questioning and doubt, Jesus still accepts him as he is. And again it's Thomas who speaks for all his companions and crystallises their conviction.

In Galilee, in what must have seemed like another age, Thomas had survived the storm on the lake with Jesus. Now the inner storm has died away, the waves of doubt that threatened to swamp him are pacified. For Thomas, this is his day of resurrection, the day he puts all the uncertainties and insecurities of his old life behind him and takes on a new assurance. And it's Thomas the seeker who at last grasps the true nature of Jesus and puts it into words.

We're not told how the rest of the disciples reacted at that moment. Were they looking at Jesus or at Thomas? Were they on their feet or on their knees? It was the defining moment of their lives. This mountain top of utter conviction might not continue into the future with this same breathtaking intensity, but its power and inspiration would fuel them through the years of witness and struggle that lay ahead.

It worked for Thomas. Just outside the city of Chennai – Madras – in South India, in the suburb of Mylapore, there's a small hill called St. Thomas' Mount. It grows out of the surrounding plain like a witness itself. I've climbed the hill and visited the small church on its summit. It's dedicated to Thomas. Ancient church history tells us that during the days of the expansion of the early Christian church Thomas travelled to India, taking the good news of Jesus with him. He attracted many believers and the Mar Thoma (Saint Thomas) Church was founded. We're also told that 20 years later, in A.D.52, he was martyred on the mount and for some time his body was buried there. When early European explorers like Vasco da Gama arrived here in the 16th century, they were surprised to find the church still flourishing. It still is today, throughout South India and in many other parts of the world where Indian Christians have gone, taking their faith with them. Not bad, for honest, doubting, questioning Thomas.

It's acceptable to ask questions. Our minds are God-given and he expects us to use them. It was a dangerous risk on God's part to give us this freedom and I wonder if he doesn't occasionally regret it. But God is tough, and loving enough to cope with our questions and hesitations. Jesus never said, "Come to me all you who have great faith" or "Come to me when you've won your battle with doubt." He said, "Come to me, all you who are weary and burdened, and I will give you rest." (Matthew 11:28) Come as you struggle with your questions. Your faith may be no bigger than a grain of mustard seed, as vulnerable as the first tiny root from the seed, but it can grow. Through questioning and doubt we can be given the grace to stand with Thomas and share his wonder and worship as we say together, "My Lord and my God!"

Yes, Lord, yes.
I see you,
holding out your hands,
creative hands,
released from saw and plane and wood,
now fashioning new life.
Hands, still scarred by suffering,
cupping the world in love
and building miracles of faith.
Hands that lit fire on the beach
set fire to hearts
to burn away
the questions and the doubt.

Lord, yes.
That's all I want to say
to all you ask.
Not knowing what the future holds
but confident you hold the future safe,
my future safe.
You are the image of the father
who stands and waits and watches
for the prodigal's return
and runs to meet him.

Yes, Lord.
I have a hope,
not lottery-ticket hope,
the odds stacked high
and heavily against me
– you are no Bingo-caller, Lord –
but hope that's strong and sure,
that tells me with a certainty I grasp in faith
that I'll be gathered into your embrace
with Thomas.

Yes, Lord.
You are the Lord of history,
the cosmos-maker,
yet in your loving-kindness
the history of my doubts and fears
is blotted out
and I am taken as I am
for what I can become.
In awe I share your resurrection
and leave the empty tomb behind
to find new life with you.
You are my way,
my truth,
my life.
You are my Lord,
my God.
Yes, and Amen.

Postscript

Five people meet Jesus and their lives are transformed, each shaped anew by their encounter. The paralysed man gains the power to walk, the freedom to make his own way in life, and recognises Jesus as the man who made him well. The blind man, his sight restored, finds the wonder of God's creation in all its colour and beauty, and the joy of independent life. The man carrying the burden of leprosy, alone, excluded from human fellowship, has his humanity restored and is brought back into the community. Mary is given new worth as a woman. She is the first to meet the Jesus of the resurrection, and is given the responsibility of sharing the breathtaking news of new life and new relationships. And Thomas? His questions and doubt are made irrelevant by the heart-stopping joy of recognising Jesus as Lord of life itself.

Each encounter encourages us to face the reality of who Jesus was, and is. A reality so great and beyond our imagining that we can only grasp a tiny fragment of the truth he embodies; we simply walk on the edge of it. That's enough to set us on our way, to entice and encourage us to greater exploration. There's a Shaker song that describes our experience. The Shakers broke away from the Quakers in the 18th century. They left England in 1774 to found new homes in the freedom of the American colonies. Their beliefs were unorthodox but their lifestyle simple, and they lived out their faith in hard-working communities. They sang:

My life goes on in endless song
above earth's lamentations,
I hear the real, though far-off hymn
that hails a new creation.

Through all the tumult and the strife
I hear its music ringing,
it sounds an echo in my soul.
How can I keep from singing?

No storm can shake my inmost calm,
while to that rock I'm clinging.
Since love is lord of heaven and earth
how can I keep from singing?

It's a song of joy and hope and trust in the goodness and love of God whatever our experience of the world suggests. A song that never ends; the only thing that will change is the place where we will sing it.

Lord, I hear the song,
your song.
Faint now and far away,
a whisper on the breeze
playing the leaves of my life,
hardly disturbing them.
But then it grows, your song,
circles the edge of my hearing,
echoes in the empty caverns of my life,
enticing,
inviting me to join the choir.
I want to sing your song,
make it my own.
A pilgrim song
which takes me on my way.

I'll sing it
when the road is clearly marked,
I'll sing it
when my feet are sore
and when my knees begin to ache.
I'll sing it breathlessly
up in the mountains
where the path is full of rocks
and I'm not sure which path to take.
I'll sing it
when the clouds roll in
and visibility is nil.
A song of joy and hope and love.
I'll sing it solo if I must
but there are times I hear your voice
and we can sing together.
Sometimes
I'll sing it loud and clear,
occasionally I'll whisper it
but, Lord,
I'll go on singing
'til the day
I sing it in your presence
loud and free,
the harmony complete.

Picture shown in colour on title page

The Leprosy Mission

Restoring health, hope and dignity

All the profits from the sale of this book are going to the work of The Leprosy Mission in hospitals and rehabilitation centres in the developing world.

Leprosy is a medical condition affecting millions of people, 90% of whom live in the developing world.

Leprosy causes disability and even blindness, if untreated, by attacking nerves under the skin, leading to loss of feeling, paralysis and unfelt injury of the hands, feet and face.

Leprosy can be cured using Multidrug therapy (MDT) in as little as six months to a year. Since the 1980s over 10 million people have been cured with MDT, but the challenge remains as over 750,000 new cases are still detected each year.

TLM Trading Limited, owned by The Leprosy Mission, seeks to create employment by purchasing goods from rehabilitation centres and craft workshops which employ people affected by leprosy. These goods are sold along with gifts, cards and books to raise funds for TLM.

If you would like information about...

- Our mail order gift catalogue
- The Leprosy Mission's work
- Prayer support
- Supporting The Leprosy Mission financially
- Service overseas with The Leprosy Mission
- Making and amending a will and leaving a legacy to TLM

Contact us on ...
Tel: 0845 166 2253 (local rate, UK only)
Email: enquiries@tlmtrading.com

OR use one of the contact addresses on the right.

Useful addresses

TLM TRADING LIMITED
To buy books, gifts and craft items made by leprosy affected people contact us at...
PO Box 212, Peterborough, PE2 5GD, UK
Tel: 01733 239252 Fax: 01733 239258
Email: enquiries@tlmtrading.com
www.tlmtrading.com

TLM INTERNATIONAL
80 Windmill Road, Brentford,
Middlesex, TW8 0QH, UK.
Tel: 020 8326 6767 Fax: 020 8326 6777
Email: friends@tlmint.org
www.leprosymission.org

TLM ENGLAND AND WALES
Channel Islands and the Isle of Man
Goldhay Way, Orton Goldhay,
Peterborough, PE2 5GZ, UK
Tel: 01733 370505 Fax: 01733 404880
Email: post@tlmew.org.uk
www.leprosymission.org.uk

TLM NORTHERN IRELAND
Leprosy House, 44 Ulsterville Avenue,
Belfast, BT9 7AQ,
Northern Ireland
Tel: 02890 381937 Fax: 02890 381842
Email: info@tlm-ni.org
www.tlm-ni.org

TLM SCOTLAND
89 Barnton Street, Stirling,
Scotland FK8 1HJ,
Tel: 01786 449 266 Fax: 01786 449 766
Email: lindatodd@compuserve.com
www.biggar-net.co.uk/tlmscotland

The Leprosy Mission has offices all around the world. Please contact TLM International if you would like contact details for any of the following offices:

Africa Regional Office, Australia, Belgium, Canada, Denmark, Finland, France, Germany, Hungary, India Regional Office, Ireland, Italy, Netherlands, New Zealand, Portugal, South-East Asia Regional Office, South Africa, Spain, Sweden, Switzerland, USA (Assoc Org), Zimbabwe

Shop online at www.tlmtrading.com